Blessed Gianna Beretta Molla

Blessed Gianna Beretta Molla

A Woman's Life

1922–1962

Giuliana Pelucchi

With a Foreword by
Antoinette Bosco

BOOKS & MEDIA
Boston

Library of Congress Cataloging-in-Publication Data

Pelucchi, Giuliana, 1928–
[Vita per la vita. English]
Blessed Gianna Beretta Molla : a woman's life, 1922–1962 / by Giuliana Pelucchi.
p. cm.
ISBN 0-8198-3099-2
1. Beretta Molla, Gianna, 1922–1962. 2. Christian woman martyrs—Italy—Biography. I. Title.
BX4700.B42 P4513 2002
282'.092—dc21

2002000535

Photos (except those of Gianna's beatification) courtesy of Pietro Molla through the kindness of Fr. Tom Rosica and *Edizioni Paoline,* Milan, Italy.

Translated by Paul Duggan

Printed and published in the U.S.A. by Pauline Books & Media, 50 Saint Pauls Avenue, Boston, MA 02130-3491.

Pauline Books & Media is the publishing house of the Daughters of St. Paul, an international congregation of women religious serving the Church with the communications media.
www.pauline.org

1 2 3 4 5 6 7 8 9 10 09 08 07 06 05 04 03 02

Contents

Foreword

It is a common expression to say someone is "a saint" even though that word is not easily defined. In the pages to come, we meet a contemporary woman who lived a life that was both ordinary and heroic, energized always by her conviction of God's love for everyone. The life of Blessed Gianna Beretta Molla underscores that sainthood was never meant to be seen in romantic terms. Being one of God's "blessed ones" takes heroic fidelity to living God's laws—and that is the person we meet on these pages.

Gianna was a woman, entirely. She liked fashionable clothes, wanted a good education, loved painting and playing the piano, chose nice furnishings for her home, enjoyed mountain climbing and skiing in the Alps, vacations in the country, and concerts. She truly loved life. But as a teenager, she also knew the tragedy of war and the pain of losing loved ones—four of her thirteen siblings and her parents died before she was twenty. She had a great commitment to her faith, a very active spiritual life of prayer and work, specifically with the St. Vincent de Paul Society, a group dedicated to helping the poor and oppressed, and Catholic Action. Her love and concern for the well being of others led her to choose medicine as her life's work and mission.

Gianna was over thirty years old when she met Pietro Molla. She must have yearned a long time for a soul mate, and clearly, Pietro fulfilled this real and strong need when he courted her. Their mutual love was intense and their marriage a joyful and fruitful union, with three babies coming quickly as they formed their family.

But all relationships have their moments of solitude. Pietro's many absences—he made frequent business trips abroad—were difficult for Gianna, as she tried to balance caring for their young children and home with a demanding medical practice. Most women in that situation would have felt anger. Maybe Gianna did. But those of us raised in the Italian culture, which is so rooted in the primacy of family connections, may have a greater understanding of her story. Having grown up myself among Italian women of her generation, I suspect that she chose what she truly considered the better way: she counted on her own strength—and God's—to keep the family going.

And she was indeed a strong woman. Gianna possessed the courage and true love necessary to put others ahead of herself. Her life experiences—family, work, marriage, motherhood—tightly wound together by her tremendous trust in God, were a training course where she made the choices that would become her biography.

And her most important choice, because of her deep love for life, was her motherhood. With her fourth pregnancy, Gianna faced the most momentous choice a person can ever confront: giving up life, if necessary, so another can live. She knew that rooted within her was the origin of another human being, and this was not her doing, but God's. Courageously, she made the only decision that she, with the beginning of new life inside her, could make. She would not have her uterus removed, the operation she needed if her own life was to be assured, because it would certainly kill the tiny child within her.

As a doctor, this mother knew what her choice might mean. It takes enormous inner strength to face the very real possibility of your own death when you also know it could be averted. As a mother, I could understand if she had wept bitterly, knowing the price she might have to pay: never to be there as her children grew. But I sense that Gianna chose to believe she would not die, and shared this optimistic view with her beloved Pietro. Even so, like Jesus, Gianna left her destiny in the hands of her Father out of love for the life within her.

Perhaps sainthood is definable after all. It's essence radiates from a life lived with courage and altruism, always putting the love of others ahead of one's own. This was the life of choices made by Gianna, a truly "Blessed" woman. In her younger years, Gianna had written, "Our task is to make the truth visible and loveable in ourselves, offering ourselves as an attractive and, if possible, heroic example." She could not have known how prophetic her words would be.

Antoinette Bosco, author

⌘ 1 ⌘

A Journalist's Task

In September of 1993, Pietro Molla called to tell me he had just received some incredible news. Reverend Paolino Rossi—the Postulator for the cause of Gianna Beretta Molla's canonization—had informed Pietro that his wife, Giannna, who had died some thirty-one years before, would be proclaimed a blessed by the Church.

Deeply moved by the emotion in his voice, I could not respond for a moment. Actually, I didn't know what to say. I tried to imagine his state of mind, to find the right words to show him how much I shared in his joy, which had come out of so much suffering.

I asked Pietro if we could meet, as we had so often while I was writing Gianna's biography. Then, we had gone over the details of her life and delved into his memories of her and their life together. I had wanted Pietro to tell me about the years following her death, years that unfolded in a reserved silence that was his way of protecting a painful yet sweet memory, which he treasured.

So much has been said and written about Gianna, who died at the age of thirty-nine after giving birth to her fourth child—about her courage, her faith, her love for life. Many have analyzed her sacrifice—risking her own life to protect that of her unborn child. Some admire her choice. Others struggle to accept it. But most agree that it was certainly an exceptional act of love, which has become all the more unusual in our own restless and indifferent age.

As I worked with Pietro to reconstruct Gianna's life, her simplicity and humanity became more apparent to me. At times, when Pietro pointed out some detail to me, his voice would break. Working closely with him was a wonderful but difficult experience. There were moments when I felt as if I was digging pitilessly into a world that belonged to him entirely. Yet, I also had the impression that he was grateful to me because I forced him to make an effort to remember the past. In writing Gianna's biography, and lovingly shedding light on her character and personality through it, I believe that, to some extent, I have restored Gianna to him.

Pietro and I had agreed to meet at his home in Milan to discuss Gianna's beatification. And in his familiar surroundings, I listened as Pietro spoke in a quiet voice. A man of indescribable serenity despite his great suffering and trials, Pietro Molla has come to terms with the death of his wife Gianna and the sudden loss of his daughter Mariolina only two years later.

Gianna with Mariolina in front of the veranda of their home in Ponte Nuovo (1957)

Pietro spoke at length about Archbishop Carlo Colombo's request to open the process of beatification for his wife.

> My decision to consent to opening the process was an agonizing one. When I was asked to give my permission in the spring of 1970, my children were still very young and could not understand what was happening. I would have preferred to keep our affairs and sorrow private. I feared that the press would intrude on our everyday lives. Nevertheless, I accepted this request as coming from God. My one concern was that those involved not speak with the media until the cause had progressed sufficiently to be firmly established.
>
> By 1973, the religious and secular media began to write more frequently and extensively about Gianna—in Italy and abroad—with great respect and admiration....
>
> I honestly do not recall having had any clashes with the media. However, reading about our family's concerns in the papers...continuously created new suffering for us, especially for my youngest daughter, which was my greatest worry.
>
> In time, my wife's story became more widely known. Some biographies were published and then translated into various languages; in Brazil, Canada, and Italy, nursery and elementary schools and many pro-life centers were dedicated in her name. It became increasingly evident that Gianna's witness was the source of great blessings for many people.
>
> We continued to receive letters from all over the world. Women from Germany and America wrote, addressing Gianna as "mother." They felt they had a friend

> in her. They confided that they turned to her in their every need and felt that she was close to them....
>
> This outpouring of love helped to ease the pain we experienced at having our intimate family matters made public; it also helped my children to understand and accept this invasion of our privacy....
>
> I have many different feelings when I think of Gianna's beatification: surprise, almost bewilderment, and gratitude to God, joy. As a wife and mother, Gianna gave the gift of herself...so I feel a kind of grateful acceptance of this gift of divine Providence, which I regard as a recognition of the innumerable unknown mothers who, like Gianna, are quietly heroic in their love and in their lives.

As I listened to Pietro, I recalled how often he had told me: "My wife had infinite faith in God, but I never realized I was living with a 'saint.' Gianna was a woman who was full of the joy of living. She loved her family, her profession as a physician. She loved her home, music, mountains, flowers...all the beautiful gifts that God has given. She seemed to me to be a completely ordinary woman, but as Archbishop Colombo has said, '...holiness does not consist of extraordinary signs. Above all, it consists of the daily acceptance of the unfathomable designs of God.'"

As we sat together, Pietro became absorbed in his own thoughts. "Within a very short time," he mused, "Gianna will be elevated to the glory of the altar."

"But," he continued, "I hope Gianna will always rest in the cemetery of her hometown, next to our daughter Mariolina, near the many women who affectionately called her 'our doctor' and who were healed by her loving care and skill. For my children, Gianna will always be a tender mother and for me, a splendid wife. I would not add anything more; if anyone must say more, let it be the Church."

Gianna's beatification would take place in April of 1994. What could Pietro, the man with whom Gianna had shared her life and love, be experiencing after such news? I asked him about his feelings.

> I have contemplated Gianna's holiness for years and, almost unconsciously, I have been preparing for this. I have accepted God's will. With the passing of time, I have overcome my great sorrow over her death.
>
> Only recently, as I looked through Gianna's belongings for something...I found a holy card in one of her prayer books with these words she wrote on the back: "Lord, let the light that has been lit in my soul never be extinguished." That light, which gladdened my life and that of my children all too briefly, now spreads like a blessing on all who have known and loved her, on all who pray to her and entrust themselves to her intercession before God. In a powerful way, this knowledge reminds me of the gift the Lord gave me in allowing me to share part of my life with Gianna.

2

A Woman Like Any Other

From the home where Pietro Molla and his small children lived after Gianna's death, one can see the small town square of Mesero lined with short, old houses. A tree grows out of a wall that surrounds a garden. Standing by the window, Pietro points out the building where Gianna had her doctor's office.

The house is still furnished with the same pieces Gianna had so lovingly chosen before her wedding. The atmosphere is bright, the rooms elegant and practical. Some silver-framed portraits, the work of a famous photographer, hang on the walls and sit on the mantel. The photographs show a happy woman surrounded by her children—Gianna with Pierluigi, then with Laura and Mariolina. There is also a small canvas portraying a house set among trees that Gianna painted—she had always loved painting. A piano stands in a corner of the room as a testimony of her passion for music. "My wife played very well," says Pietro. "Her mother taught her when she was a child."

While Gianna was still alive, the family lived in Ponte Nuovo, in Magenta. Their villa was located in the neighborhood where Pietro, an engineer, managed the factory known as La Saffa. The church where Gianna prayed whenever she had a free moment is only a short distance from their villa.

Pietro showed me around the house before leading me into his study where we sat surrounded by the books and folders containing the documents of Gianna's life, which she spent in the daily acceptance of God's will.

Pietro lowered his voice, as people tend to do when discussing something deeply personal. His memory of the incidents that took place long ago is clear—printed indelibly on his heart.

"Gianna was a splendid, but ordinary woman," he says, in measured words. "She was stylish and elegant, a beautiful and intelligent woman who loved to smile. She loved going to the mountains and she skied very well. She loved music. For years, we had season tickets for the concerts at the Milan Conservatory. Since we had to travel to Milan from our home in Ponte Nuovo," he says with a smile, "we usually skipped supper so that we wouldn't miss a minute of the concert. She also liked to travel. Because I had to make business trips abroad, we went together as much as possible. We went to Holland, Germany, Sweden, England. We spent some time in places all over Europe...."

While I listened, I could not help asking Pietro, once again, what Gianna was *really* like—that woman who was a dedicated wife, mother, and physician, who loved life so

Gianna in Taormina, Sicily, during her honeymoon

much and yet who was willing to sacrifice it with incredible generosity.

> Beyond any doubt, Gianna was a happy woman. She was like any other woman, but she possessed something more: a profound religious spirit and an indomitable faith in God. She never wavered in her faith, not even during the last months of her life.
>
> Gianna was a competent physician and she knew that she would probably not survive the birth of the baby she was expecting. But she never lost hope that God would save them both. For instance, there was a little episode that might seem trivial to others, but is quite significant to me. Shortly before the birth of our baby in March, I had to go to Paris for a business trip. Gianna asked me to bring back some fashion magazines saying, "If God keeps me here, I would like to make some nice clothes."

Pietro took two magazines from the bookcase to show me. "Look," he said, pointing, "here are the marks she put next to the items she especially liked."

He fell silent, slowly paging through the glossy magazines. Then he put them back on the shelf.

> I am certain that the sacrifice she accepted with so much love and self-giving cost her dearly. Gianna loved living. She wasn't some mystical type who always thought of heaven and who lived on earth believing it to be, above all, a vale of tears. Rather, Gianna was a woman who could take pleasure in the small and great joys God grants us even in this world.
>
> Nevertheless, she did not hesitate when she learned of the large tumor that threatened the normal development

of her pregnancy. Her first reaction was to ask the doctors to save the child in her womb. They advised her on her three options for surgery: a total laparotomy, which would certainly have saved her life, but would have involved the removal of both the tumor and the uterus; the termination of the pregnancy by therapeutic abortion and removal of the tumor, which would have allowed her to have other children; or the removal of just the tumor in an attempt to save the current pregnancy. Gianna chose the last option—the riskiest for herself. It was obvious that giving birth after this kind of surgery could be very dangerous—something which Gianna clearly understood.

But her decision was certainly not suicidal. As I said, Gianna trusted in God. Her choice was consistent with her whole life; it was a choice with roots reaching back to her childhood, to the profoundly religious atmosphere in which her family always lived. Her decision was rooted in her parents' example of love, which was a constant strength and security even in the most difficult times of life. Her experiences as a member of Catholic Action and the Society of St. Vincent de Paul helped to refine her spirituality and made her a generous woman—a mother to all. Her life was entirely based on this complete dedication of herself to others, up to her final sacrifice. Gianna never expected anything in return; she did not give freely "in order to go to heaven." She did it because she was a mother.

To understand her decision one must keep in mind, in the first place, Gianna's deep conviction, as a mother and a physician, that the baby she carried was a complete human being, with the same rights as any of her other children, even if conceived only two months earlier. A gift from God, this child's life deserved sacred respect. Secondly,

Gianna had great love for her children: she loved them more than she loved herself. And one cannot forget her strong trust in God. She knew how vital she was to my life and to the lives of our children, but even more, she knew that she was especially indispensable to the little child developing in her womb. Perhaps, without her unconditional trust in God, she would have made a different choice. But she was sure God would do what was best for her in the mysterious plan of his love.

3

A Serene Family Life

Gianna Beretta Molla's parents were both from the region of Lombardy in Italy. Alberto Beretta was born in Magenta on September 23, 1881; Maria De Micheli was born in Milan on May 23, 1887. Both grew up in very large families that were deeply Christian.

Alberto, the seventh boy in the Beretta family, lost his mother when he was only four. As soon as he was old enough, he went to the College of San Carlo, a boarding school in Milan. Because of the long years he spent at school, a lack of familial affection marked his childhood and youth. While still a boy, he vowed that if he ever married and had children, he would make any sacrifice to ensure that his children would grow up surrounded by the warmth of familial love.

When Alberto was in his twenties, he met Maria De Micheli, a beautiful young woman who was very religious, firm, and serene in character. They were married at St. Bartholomew's Church in Milan, on October 12, 1908.

Their children fondly recall a story their mother told them. When she was newly married, among the many wedding cards and gifts the bride received there was a particularly amusing one from a dear friend, which pictured a large wash-tub filled with thirteen children and beneath the picture the words: "your choice."

With happiness Maria immediately said, "I want them all!" And God did indeed give the Beretta family thirteen children.

The newlyweds rented an apartment in Milan on the Piazza Risorgimento, not far from a Capuchin Monastery. Both Alberto and Maria were Franciscan Tertiaries, and for as long as they lived in Milan they remained close in trust and "spiritual collaboration" with the friars.

Alberto worked for the Cantoni Cotton Company for thirty-eight years and his brilliant career led to high managerial positions. Because of his success, the Beretta home enjoyed a certain level of comfort, though always tempered by a Franciscan spirit of poverty, which the parents impressed on their children. Their strong faith helped the Berettas through difficult times of suffering, especially during World War I and the Spanish Influenza epidemic, which claimed three of their children. Alberto and Maria relied on God to assist them in everything.

In 1925, Gianna's parents decided to move to Bergamo in the hope that the children would be safer from the very serious risk of contracting the Spanish Influenza. They bought a large house surrounded by a beautiful garden in Cittá Alta, on Borgo Canale. The family lived in this house until 1937, when the illness of one of their daughters caused them to move again, this time to Genova-Quinto, near the ocean.

Only two years after moving there, World War II began. After the naval bombardment of Genove-Quinto by the English in 1941, the Berettas returned to Bergamo and moved into the old home of Maria's parents in San Vigilio where Alberto and Maria died in 1942.

As light shines through the large window facing the hills of Cittá Alta in Bergamo, Gianna's two brothers, Father Giuseppe and Father Alberto (baptized Enrico), and her older sister Zita, share memories of their family with me. We sit comfortably in the old country house of the family's maternal grandparents, nestled in the meadows and vineyards of San Vigilio—one of the loveliest spots in Bergamo.

Father Giuseppe calmly tells of the family's joys and sorrows, of the serene and dramatic moments that followed each other through the quickly passing years.

Zita and Father Alberto listen quietly to their brother. Now and then Zita speaks to dwell a bit longer on a particularly memorable event. Father Alberto, unable to speak because of paralysis, nods his head in approval as the stories unfold.

And, once again, I find myself immersed in the peaceful atmosphere of an acceptance of God's plans joined with conviction and deep commitment to living the Christian faith. "Our parents," Father Giuseppe says, "were two extraordinary people. Every day we thank the Lord for having had such a wonderful father and mother. They were filled with true spiri-

Maria and Alberto Beretta (1933)

Gianna at age 11

tuality. They had a religious view of life, but they remained down-to-earth—after all, my mother did have to raise thirteen children!

> Our little brother David wrote an essay, "My Family" when he was in elementary school, in which he said, "My mother is a wet nurse." This regional expression meant that our mother always had a small baby in her arms. She nursed us all, my mother did. And she was the one who got us dressed every morning until we were in the fifth grade.
>
> We lived in Milan at the time of the Spanish Influenza epidemic, and it struck hard in our home: first our brother David died, then our sister Pierina, then another little sister, Rosina. In addition, Amalia, who was sixteen years old, had the beginning stages of tuberculosis. My parents did not know what else to do except to leave Milan and move to Bergamo. They chose to go to Bergamo Alta because our grandparents' house was there and they were convinced that the air would be healthier. They bought a house with a large garden in Borgo Canale where both Guglielmina and Anna Maria were born and died in infancy.
>
> We lived in Borgo Canale for twelve years, until Gianna was about fifteen years old. Papa commuted from Bergamo to Milan every day by train.
>
> Together, our parents made each other whole. Every morning, they would rise very early in the morning to go to the first Mass in the church of Borgo Canale. They loved each other very much. I believe that when they married they must have asked God to let them die together. They could not even imagine living without each other. On April 28, 1942, something incredible happened. Papa told Mama that he felt very ill. "I am dying, Maria," he insisted.

> Mama studied him carefully and then said, "That isn't possible. I'm fine. I don't feel a thing." But that evening, my mother had a heart attack and passed away the next day.
>
> Papa died only four months later. He was never the same after Mama's death. We helped him in every possible way, practically forcing him to live. He had cerebral anemia and refused to feed himself.

Father Giuseppe fell silent for a while and then, as if emerging from a distant world, continued to reminisce.

> Gianna was born in Magenta on October 4, 1922. On April 4, 1928, she received her First Communion in the parish of Santa Grata in Bergamo. Two years later, she was confirmed at the Cathedral. From the day of her First Communion, even while still quite young, Gianna went to Mass with Mama every day and received Holy Communion. She was a daily communicant her whole life.

Sister Virginia, or Ginia as she is affectionately called, is the youngest of the Beretta children. Virginia and Zita were closest to Gianna. Zita often acted as the "assistant mother" to Gianna and Virginia, the youngest girls of the household. Only three years apart, Gianna and Virginia shared a bedroom. They studied, played, laughed, and joked together. Above all, they dedicated themselves to following the example of their parents in living a truly Christian life.

As we sat in the little parlor of the Institute of the Canossian Sisters in Ottavia, a village just outside of Rome,

Sister Virginia recalled her childhood for me. Sister Virginia bears a strong physical resemblance to Gianna; she is a tall woman with a lovely face, broad forehead, and dark, intelligent eyes. Sister Virginia worked in India and Hong Kong for many years as a medical missionary. Now she works among the people of Rome with the same self-giving dedication and enthusiasm she exhibited in the missions. Her memories of Gianna are full of affection and loving admiration. She considers it a gift from God that she was able to stay in the hospital with Gianna during the last, painful days of her life.

> Gianna had great enthusiasm for life. She loved and enjoyed everything good that can be found in the world. We often went mountain climbing during our vacations. We loved the fresh air of the hills around Bergamo and we took many long walks together not only on vacations, but also on Sundays.
>
> We went to school together, and Gianna would help me do my homework. We frequently had the same teachers and, therefore, the same little problems. We studied wherever we pleased: in our bedroom, in the dining room, or in the garden if the weather was nice. Because we both had the habit of saying our lessons aloud, we had to try not to annoy each other.

When I asked about Gianna's physical problems during her last pregnancy, Sister Virginia became more reflective.

> I had received a letter from her some time before I returned to Italy from the missions. In her letter, she told me about some complications she was experiencing, but did not go into details. Actually, she assured me that the pregnancy

was going well. When I arrived at the port in Naples, Francesco met me and informed me of Gianna Emanuela's birth and of Gianna's serious condition. We left Naples immediately and, after a brief stopover in Rome, reached Monza on Tuesday. My sister died on Saturday. I spent the last four days of her life by her side.

Gianna remained lucid almost until the end. The moment I entered her hospital room, even before greeting me, she looked directly at me and said, "If you only knew what it means to die leaving four children behind!"

At this point, I raised the objection frequently voiced by people with regard to Gianna's decision: Was it fair to abandon her three children in order to save one? Sister Virginia's answer was firm:

In order to be able to understand Gianna's decision, one must believe, as she did, in God's love. As we were growing up our mother often repeated this old, Italian proverb to us: "Every baby is born with a loaf of bread under its arm" that is, with the gift of life, God provides all that is necessary. Gianna was convinced that God would provide for all of her children. She truly loved and respected the child she was carrying in her womb...Gianna trusted in God.

It was difficult for me to walk into the hospital in Monza, having just come from my work in the interior of India in a hospital without electricity or drinking water—I felt like I was walking into a palace. "Think of what they can do here to save you with all this equipment," I told her. Yet, even with all the advanced treatments, they could not help her.

When I asked Sister Virginia why she believed Gianna was a saint, she thought for a moment. Then, looking at me, she answered:

> It is not only the great generosity of her action that marked her end, but the fact that she did the Lord's will each day in whatever situation she found herself. Her ability to make that ultimate decision was simply the result of an entire lifetime of holiness. Gianna possessed a spirit of great faith; she accepted whatever happened to her as a gift from the hands of God. From childhood, she would talk about how we should always do our best in everything, without ever hesitating or retreating. She lived her life doing God's will in everyday things: her household tasks, her studies, her profession. She lived the will of God in the gift of herself to the poor, to young people, to her children, and to her husband Pietro. Gianna did everything very quietly and willingly. Holiness, after all, consists in carrying out one's responsibilities well.

On October 12, 1933, a family portrait was taken for the twenty-fifth wedding anniversary of Maria and Alberto Beretta. From left to right, front: Gianna, her mother Maria, Virginia, Amalia, Alberto, and Giuseppe. Back: Francesco, Ferdinando, Zita, and Enrico

⫷ 4 ⫸

Fascism in Bergamo

Ferdinando, or Nando, the third of the Beretta brothers, currently lives in Magenta where he is a physician. The memory of Gianna remains very much alive for him. In his mind's eye, he sees her as a happy young girl in the large house on Borgo Canale; he remembers her little pranks and the sound of their mother scolding Gianna as she pronounced her name, syllable by syllable: "Gi-a-nna, come here!"

"Gianna and Virginia were always together," he said, "cheerful and imaginative in their games. They were very attached to our mother and, being full of curiosity, they continually asked her the most amusing questions. In 1928, when Gianna was six years old, our parents enrolled her in the first grade at Colle Aperto. Every morning, accompanied by our housekeeper or one of us older children, she walked to school wearing her neat pinafore and carrying her books in a bag. I don't know if she felt very excited about her new life as a student," Ferdinando smiled. "She, like many of her classmates, did her work willingly enough, but it was clear to me that she would have preferred to play in the garden with her dear Ginia.

> In Italy, those were the years under fascism, and at home we older ones discussed politics rather heatedly. At suppertime, our table tended to be rather noisy. Once, two women happened to be walking by our house during one of our discussions and heard us shouting. They stopped and commented, "The Berettas are quarreling!"
>
> Papa and Mama were very attentive with regard to our religious education. Yet, they left us free to learn for ourselves the value of what they taught. Enrico [Father Alberto] was the liveliest one among us. During his third year of high school, each Sunday after Mass he made sure to finish studying as soon as possible so that he could go right after dinner to the cinema in Lower Bergamo, which featured a number of films. He would entertain himself there until after the last show. From time to time we boys, with some companions from the university, would organize our own performances—some of them were quite well done and made us especially proud.
>
> We did everything we could to avoid participating in the programs organized by the fascists. We had the required uniforms, but we tried to keep them in the closet as much as possible. If it couldn't be avoided, we went to the meetings—the "fascist sabbath"—where a roll call was taken. When we heard our names we answered with the usual "present" and then, as soon as possible, slipped through the first door we could find and headed elsewhere. This certainly did not please some of our "comrades" who looked unfavorably on us and treated us with no small mistrust.

Gianna was too young to realize what was happening during that period. After completing the first grade at Colle Aperto, Gianna attended the second and third grades in a school run by the Sisters of Wisdom located right on the train line linking the Upper City (Cittá Alta) with the Lower City (Cittá Bassa) of Bergamo. During Gianna's last two years of elementary school, she and Virginia were enrolled at the Institute of the Canossian Mothers of St. Gotthard, only a short distance from home.

Gianna passed her exam for entrance into the Paolo Scarpi Lyceum secondary school. However, she was held back a few months because of poor marks in physical education—perhaps a small retaliation against the Beretta family on the part of the fascists. However, no one thought twice about it at home.

That same year, 1933, the family was preparing for an important celebration: the twenty-fifth wedding anniversary of Alberto and Maria. A photograph taken on that day shows the couple surrounded by their children: the sweet-tempered Maria, the upright, stern Alberto wearing a fine mustache, Gianna and Virginia (Ginia) dressed in identical outfits made by their mother, Amalia, Giuseppe, Francesco (Cecco), Ferdinando (Nando), and Zita.

Gianna's first four years of secondary school were uneventful. Some of her classmates remember her as a quiet, disciplined, and kind girl. She was not especially brilliant in her studies and, due to her frail health, found study an effort. In her third year, she was held back in Italian and Latin and, while the family went to Viggiona for vacation, she had to

The athletic Gianna pausing on the brow of a mountain during a climb (1952)

spend part of the summer in Bergamo studying for her makeup exams.

Between translating Latin (under the direction of Father Emilio Rota), and writing essays in Italian, Gianna wrote amusing and ingenuous letters to her family. She wrote to her Nando, who was doing military service in the province of Le Marche, and to her mother, father, and sisters who were already on vacation. Alone in Bergamo, Gianna felt rather impatient and restless, and she suffered terribly from the heat. The lessons were difficult and, as she wrote to her brother, she often found someone who easily convinced her to abandon her already weak resolve not to waste time in useless chatter. Finally, after passing her exams, Gianna escaped to the mountains to enjoy some carefree days of vacation with her family.

During her fourth year of secondary school, Gianna's oldest sister, Amalia, died at the age of twenty-six after a long illness. It was a sorrowful event for everyone, but the loss was particularly difficult for Gianna. She suddenly encountered the world of suffering, but through this suffering, her faith seemed to grow stronger. Sister Virginia remembers Gianna "reaching out to heaven" during this time:

> Every morning she would spend some time in meditation—even briefly when pressed for time. This practice became her strength. In the afternoon, she would stop at a church for a visit to the Blessed Sacrament. She always kept a rosary in her pocket or purse, and prayed some Hail Marys whenever she could.

In 1937, Alberto Beretta, who was already ill with pernicious anemia, decided to retire after a lifetime of working at the Cantoni Cotton Mills in Milan. He also decided that it was time for the family to leave Bergamo Alta. Zita, Francesco, Ferdinando, and Enrico were all enrolled in the university. Gianna was still feeling somewhat listless after Amalia's death. Alberto and Maria found a house in Genova-Quinto, a seaside city and university center. This enabled the children to remain at home while attending classes.

∝ 5 ∝

Gianna's Youth and Ideals

The years in Genova-Quinto were fundamental for Gianna's formation. When the Berettas settled into their new house near the sea, Gianna was a reserved fifteen-year-old girl in search of her life's direction. Amalia's death had truly hit her hard. She had been very fond of Amalia, in whom she had always confided her troubles, and she missed her big sister's affection. Gianna tried to follow the example Amalia had given her and to find the strength to be worthy of having such a sister.

After Amalia's death, Gianna's affection for Virginia became even stronger. The two girls enrolled in the secondary school run by the Dorothean Sisters. Every morning they went to Mass in the church near their house. They studied diligently and helped each other to earn good grades.

In the spring of Gianna's fifth year of secondary school [corresponding to our second year of high school], a Jesuit priest named Father Michele Avedano gave a retreat for the students of the school. The two Beretta girls followed the spiritual exercises with special devotion. Gianna kept a book of notes from the conferences, and she wrote down the resolutions the talks inspired. The retreat marked an important moment in Gianna's life as Monsignor Antonio Rimoldi, Gianna's official biographer, states: "This was essential for her spiritual growth. By carefully reading her notes, we can see the outline of her future conduct."

At the beginning of her notebook, Gianna wrote the words: "Notes and Prayers of Gianna Beretta," and the date: "March 16–18, 1938." After each set of conference notes, she added prayers—which she recited faithfully—to Jesus, to Our Lady and, in particular, a prayer to Christ seeking his Divine will and the grace of enlightened trust. The prayer begins in this way: "Jesus, I promise to submit to everything that you will allow to happen to me. Only help me to know your will."

Her innocent and simple words show how seriously Gianna engaged in the spiritual exercises. From her resolutions, it is also possible to perceive how the young girl was beginning to form the ideals she would strive to live. She wished to offer everything to Jesus, both sufferings and joys; to die rather than commit serious sin; to pray; to learn to trust God in the trials and sufferings of life; to accept his will; and, finally, to seek to know the unfathomable designs of Providence.

As the first step in her new "program of life," Gianna decided to dedicate herself completely to "her work," that is, her studies. As a result, she finished that scholastic year with exceptional grades.

Notwithstanding this change, Alberto and Maria decided to withdraw their daughter from school for a time. Because

buon viaggio al mio papà; papà torna presto, papà carissimo – Ma... la lontananza è sempre lontananza –
Ieri sera alla TV. Padre Mariano parlando del vero Amore del Matrimonio diceva che "il vero amore, è l'amore che non dura un solo giorno, ma sempre" e due sposi che sempre si sono amati, quando saranno in Paradiso s'accorgeranno che il tempo che si son voluti bene è stato breve e godranno nel pensare che hanno tutta l'eternità dinanzi a loro, per continuare ad amarsi –
Pedrin d'or, tu sai quanto ti amo, ti penso e ti desidero felice –
Torna presto ad abbracciarci. Tanti tanti bacioni dai tuoi tesori.

Un abbraccio affettuosissimo
dalla tua Gianna

One of the many letters Gianna wrote to maintain strong ties with family and friends

Gianna's health was still rather frail, they worried about the strain of her scholastic work. Their hope was that a rest before facing the rigors of the final years of high school would benefit her.

It was a peaceful year for Gianna. She accepted the suspension of her studies, happy to be able to enjoy the uninterrupted presence of her mother. She took pleasure in helping her mother make the home ever more comfortable for her brothers and sisters. During that year, Gianna also cultivated her passion for the piano, which she practiced every day.

Under the guidance of Monsignor Mario Righetti, the pastor and well-known liturgist of Quinto al Mare, Gianna's spirituality deepened. Following the example of her mother, who had accepted the pastor's request to become the president of Catholic Women despite her many duties as the mother of a large family, Gianna joined the Young Girls of Catholic Action and later became a delegate.

The significance of Gianna's participation is evident in a note written some fifteen years later by Monsignor Righetti: "Dear Gianna, as I am always mindful of and thankful for the examples of genuine Christian life given by you and your loved ones in Quinto...."

In October 1939, Gianna resumed her studies at the Institute of the Dorothean Sisters, at Genova Albaro.

6

War and Death

As the 1940s approached, war was in the air. Everyone realized that years of suffering lay not too far ahead. Alberto and Maria Beretta watched their children grow up and set out on their own. Gianna and Virginia were attending high school in Albaro, while their brothers and sister all enrolled at the University of Genoa. Francesco and Giuseppe were pursuing degrees in engineering, Ferdinando and Enrico in medicine, and Zita was studying to become a pharmacist.

In 1941, Genoa was one of the first cities in Italy to suffer the agony of World War II. An attack from sea shook its foundations and resulted in the first civilian casualties and the destruction of many buildings. It was a terrible time. Maria Beretta, whose heart was already weak, felt the affects of the devastation in a particularly strong way. The family decided to take her away from that place of peril and fear.

By midsummer, the Beretta family had managed to reach Viggiona, the village on Lake Maggiore where they had spent many happy vacations together. Then, in October, Alberto and Maria moved back to Bergamo, this time to the house on the hill of San Vigilio belonging to Maria's parents. Virginia and Gianna returned to Genoa in the fall with the family housekeeper, Marietta, to continue their studies.

Meanwhile, Ferdinando had been drafted into the army and was serving as a medical officer at Taggia, not far from the border of Italy and France. Francesco had obtained his engineering degree and worked in a Milanese factory. Zita, now a pharmacist, was working in San Giovanni Bianco in the province of Bergamo. Only Enrico and Giuseppe remained in San Vigilio with their parents; they had transferred to the University of Pavia and were studying for their examinations at home.

All of the brothers and sisters were very worried about their father; he suffered intensely from his pernicious anemia, which had begun to grow worse. Although very troubled by her husband's condition, Maria held the threads of her large, scattered family together. She prayed for her children who were far away and for her husband whose mental awareness had diminished because of his illness. Maria emerged from each new difficulty with the faith and courage that was always an example for her children.

Giuseppe recalls how, on the evening of April 28, 1942:

> Our mother was suddenly stricken by a cerebral ictus. Papa was ill in his room, unaware of what was happening. Fortunately, Ferdinando came back the next day on a furlough from the front. We were the only ones home, because Enrico had some sort of meeting. We quickly realized the seriousness of the situation. Ferdinando treated Mama and she was able to rally for a time. She even recognized Enrico

when he came back. "Don't worry about me," she told him. "Go and take care of Papa." But she was getting worse. We managed to telephone Zita and asked her to come back from San Giovanni. The following morning, Mama died of a heart attack.

We tried to telephone Gianna and Virginia, but communication was difficult during the war, and we were not able to contact them. Enrico wanted to bring them home, so he hurried to the station in the hope of finding a train to Genoa. He left that evening, but it was a dreadful trip. The train kept stopping—it seemed as if it would never arrive. Genoa had been bombed again; many houses had been destroyed and fires still blazed. With his heart full of sadness, Enrico finally arrived in Quinto and told our sisters about Mama.

The three of them found a train to return to Bergamo. After a hazardous trip, they finally reached San Vigilio. But by the time they arrived home, it was too late—Mama had died a few hours earlier. I remember how strange the weather was that spring. The fruit trees—cherry, peach, and pear—were already flowering, but it was snowing; large flakes were falling and the hills were covered in white.... Mama's death was a great sorrow for us all, tempered only by faith. Our sadness drew us even closer together as brothers and sisters.

Several days after Maria Beretta's funeral, Gianna returned to Genoa to finish school. In June of 1942, at the age of twenty, she earned her classical diploma without taking exams, which were postponed because of the war.

On September 1, four months after the death of his wife, Alberto Beretta died surrounded by his children.

Not long after their father's death, Giuseppe told his brothers and sisters about a desire that had been growing in his heart: he wanted to become a priest. He had already discussed his vocation with the bishop of Bergamo, Adriano Bernareggi, who had advised Giuseppe to take his theology courses even before finishing his degree in engineering. Then, around the same time, Enrico announced that he too felt called to the priesthood. He dreamed of going to the missions and serving the most needy people as a physician.

"In October," remembers Zita, "they both left. Giuseppe entered the seminary in Bergamo as the bishop had advised, and Enrico, who was already a doctor, entered the Capuchins at Lovere to begin his novitiate. Gianna enrolled as a medical student at the university in Milan. Virginia went to Monza to finish school at the Biancone.... It was time for us to move once again and we all decided that we would put our roots in Magenta, where our father had been born. The house belonging to our paternal grandparents was empty and it became our permanent residence. The relocation from Quinto to Magenta was very hard—it was certainly not the best of times to undertake such a move. Nevertheless, we succeeded in transporting all our belongings safely to Magenta. Francesco, the oldest, became the head of the family."

Trials were by no means over for the family. Ferdinando was imprisoned in a concentration camp. Enrico was drafted into military service while in the novitiate in Lovere and had to attend a school for medical officers in Florence. But after receiving word of Italy's surrender to the Allies, he took refuge in Viggiona and then secretly went into exile in Switzer-

Standing on the terrace of the house of San Vigilio, Bergamo, are Gianna Emanuela with her uncles: Father Giuseppe and Father Alberto; and her aunts: Zita and Mother Virginia

land where he attended the theological college in Fribourg. Under considerable risk, Gianna traveled back and forth between home and school in Milan. Zita bravely took on the role of mother, holding the family together in spirit. Surely, the Beretta family believed, the war had to end sometime; better days could not be far off.

7

Catholic Action and Vocation

Gianna lived in the old house on Via Roma in Magenta until she married Pietro Molla on September 24, 1955. The years between 1942 and 1955 were the most important for her spiritual and charitable maturation.

Gianna's involvement in Catholic Action began in 1944, when she was a delegate of the Benjamin [Youngest] Girls until 1945; she was a delegate of the Aspirants from 1945 to 1946, and president of Young Women from 1946 to 1949. In 1952 she again held the position of delegate, this time of the Young Girls, and from 1952 to 1955 she was again president of Young Women. During this period, she instituted the "Cenacle of the Aspirants" within Catholic Action. This was a group of girls committed to being true apostles. She organized weekly meetings in order for them to discuss topics such as prayer, grace, and the Eucharist. In fact, her apostolate among the young women whom she sought to involve in Catholic Action developed around these three basic themes. She taught them the truths of Christian doctrine, using simple explanations everyone could understand.

Photos of Dr. Beretta with children participating in the Parish Camp of Magenta Ameno in Lago d'Orta (1950)

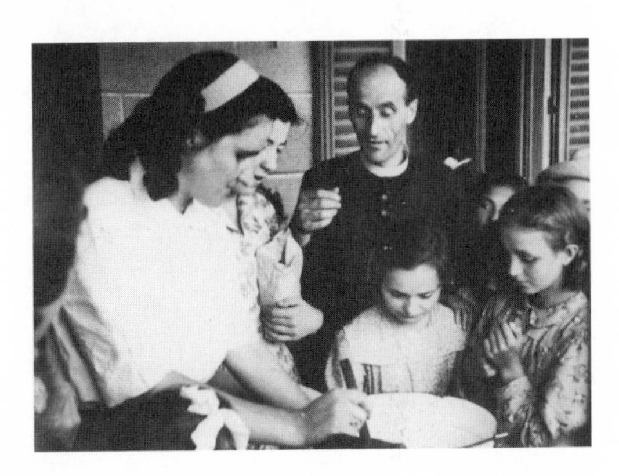

"We are apostles," she emphasized, "and if we do not want our work to be in vain, but to be effective, there is only one method that will not fail: prayer. We must pray with faith, hope, charity, humility, devotion, and reverence." She explained how "work can be prayer...if we offer to the Lord all the actions that we perform, so that they might serve his glory. Whatever we say or do should be done in the name of our Lord Jesus Christ, giving thanks to God the Father through him."

Gianna offered her own program of spiritual life in a conference to the Young Women in Magenta:

Morning and evening prayer, done properly—not in bed, but kneeling and in recollection.

Holy Mass, an irreplaceable practice. Incomparable.

Holy Communion, possibly. Maximum freedom: one who feels to and one who understands what it means should receive it.

Meditation, at least ten minutes.

Visit to the Blessed Sacrament.

Holy Rosary: without Our Lady's help no one enters Paradise.

In the collection of her writings presented to the Congregation for the Causes of Saints, some phrases reveal Gianna's constant personal ascent toward holiness, which was what she desired her girls to "try" and "taste."

> The most essential condition for every fruitful activity is stillness in prayer. The apostle begins work by kneeling. An

> apostle should never let a single day go by without including time for recollection at the feet of God. Before acting, we lift our souls to God. The more we feel the desire to give, the more often it is necessary to go back to the infinite fountain of love that is God....
>
> Our task is to make the truth visible and lovable in ourselves, offering ourselves as an attractive and, if possible, heroic example. The person who needs to touch and to feel in order to believe will not be easily won by words. Talk alone does not attract, but "making things visible" does.
>
> Work and sacrifice yourself only for the glory of God. Sow your little seeds tirelessly. If, even after all of your best efforts, failure seems to be the result, accept this generously. A failure gracefully accepted by an apostle, who has used all the means available to succeed, may be more beneficial for salvation than a victory. Let us always work generously and humbly; let us try not to look immediately for the fruits of our labor. Working not sleeping is what counts. Remember that saving the world has never been easy, not even for the Son of God, not even for the Apostles; "Catholic Action" is sacrifice.

Gianna had enrolled in medical school in Milan toward the end of 1942—that terrible year marked by the death of her parents. It seemed to her that the best way to exercise her desire to give and to ease other's pain was in becoming a doctor.

Despite the inevitable hardships connected with wartime, Gianna threw herself into her studies. Often, attending classes was nearly impossible, since Milan was under constant heavy attack. Everything was in a state of confusion. The frequent bombings destroyed buildings, and people fled the city for safer places. Gianna endured the tragedy of war with her customary intensity of life and deep faith in God. If she could not perform heroic deeds, she would strive to do whatever task was set before her as well as she could. She studied medicine and dedicated whatever time she had to the education of "her girls" and helping those who were worse off than she and her family.

When the war ended in 1945, Gianna continued her studies in the medical school in Pavia. She and Virginia, who had enrolled in the same school of medicine, rented a room in the city. Gianna believed that the medical profession was like no other; she had very clear ideas about the purpose and sanctity of her vocation and wrote some of her thoughts in her personal notes:

> In one way or another, everyone in the world works in the service of humanity. The physician works directly with the human person. The object of our science and work is the human person who is before us, who tells us about him or herself, who asks for help, and who expects from us the fullness of his or her existence.
>
> Physicians have opportunities that a priest does not have, for our mission does not end when medicine is no longer of help. There still remains the soul that must be brought to God. Jesus says, "Whoever visits the sick is helping me." This is a priestly mission! Just as the priest can touch Jesus, so we doctors touch Jesus in the bodies of our patients: in the poor, the young, the old, children....

> May Jesus reveal himself through us; may he find many physicians who willingly offer themselves to him.

On November 30, 1949, Gianna finished medical school with honors and she invited a group of her friends over to celebrate this milestone in her life. A little over two years later, on July 7, 1952, she gained her specialization in pediatrics.

Gianna moved in with Zita and Francesco who began his civil engineering after the war. Gianna opened her practice with Ferdinando who had begun his own medical practice in Mesero, a little village on the outskirts of Magenta. Every morning, whatever the weather conditions (this part of Lombardy, bordering the province of Ticino in Switzerland, is covered in a thick fog most of the year), she would leave Magenta for Mesero in her Fiat 500 to put herself at the service of her "dear patients."

In the meantime, many changes had taken place in the Beretta family. In June 1946, Bishop Bernareggi ordained Giuseppe in Bergamo. In 1948, the Capuchin, Cardinal Schuster of Grajau, Brazil, ordained Enrico (now Alberto in memory of his father) for that diocese. Father Alberto would finally fulfill his calling to be a medical missionary among the poorest people of the Brazilian northeast.

Ferdinando married Laura Viola in 1950. Virginia completed her studies in medicine in 1951 and, at last, followed the path to which God had called her: she entered the Sisters of the Congregation of Magdalene of Canossa. She soon left for India to work as a medical missionary.

Though far away, Father Alberto kept in touch with the family through regular correspondence. His letters from Brazil were full of news that could have been a source of discouragement, but he seemed hopeful. Grajau was located near the equator and the most accessible, inhabited area was hundreds of kilometers away. The heat was terrible; the people, *campesinos* and *indios,* lived in extreme poverty, their days filled with labor and misery; there was no health facility; both missionaries and supplies were greatly needed. Moreover, the Brazilian government did not recognize his Italian medical diploma and license. Father Alberto had to study and retake nearly all the examinations he had already passed with flying colors in Italy.

Gianna eagerly read all the news she received from afar and posed endless questions in her own letters. Her brother's great tranquility and courage in the face of so many difficult situations impressed her.

In one of his letters, Father Alberto, with the support of the Capuchin superiors, invited Francesco to travel to Grajau to investigate the possibility of building a small hospital. Francesco accepted. He closed his engineering office indefinitely and went to Brazil. In all, he stayed for more than two years.

Busy as she was with her practice and Catholic Action, Gianna never interrupted her correspondence with her brothers. She was so close to Francesco and Father Alberto that she almost felt she shared in their life experiences in Brazil. She was interested in the construction of the hospital and in the health conditions among the poor. It saddened her to hear that children were dying because there were no means to provide sufficient health care.

Letters also reached Gianna from India, where Sister Virginia was working as a doctor in a small leprosarium. An entirely unknown world was opening up to Gianna. She was a physician. Could the missions also be her vocation?

✤ 8 ✤

In Search of Her Own Way

Gianna's attraction for the missions only increased with each letter from Grajau. She wanted to go to Brazil to work among the *campesinos* with her brother, who was their only physician. The atmosphere in which she had always lived also fostered her "vocation," the seeds of which were planted during the 1938 spiritual exercises. The missions were not only an important part of her family life, but also a key element in Catholic Action, whose ideals included "apostolic action."

When Francesco arrived in Grajau to build the hospital, he encountered considerable difficulties, not least of which were economic. Gianna sought to help her brothers from Magenta with prayer and fund-raising. She was diligent and loving in the practice of her profession as a doctor among the people of Mesero, but she continued to imagine herself in that distant land where she was sure she could do so much more good. She especially longed to help the poor *campesino* mothers and their children. As a woman she felt that she was better suited for this work than her brother.

It seems that Gianna may have even gone to the medical school in Milan to get information on obtaining a specialization in obstetrics and gynecology. Although she did not pursue this, she wrote to her brother and informed him that she hoped to be able to accompany Father Cecilio, a Capuchin from Milan, leaving soon for Brazil. She wanted to learn first-hand what life was like in Grajau. "What do you think? I have not yet found a substitute for my practice in Mesero, but I always hope that the Lord will provide someone at the right time. I am studying a little Portuguese; then, if God wills, I would be very happy to come. Pray that everything goes well...." In another letter she wrote, "Here everything seems fine, and I am waiting for you to tell me when I should come down there...." Obviously, Brazil had a strong hold on her heart.

When Gianna discussed her tentative plans with Father Giuseppe, he, in turn, spoke with Bishop Bernareggi for some insight on the matter. He told the bishop about the rough conditions in Grajau and about Gianna's inability to endure the tropical heat. Indeed, Father Giuseppe remembers that, "When it got hot, Gianna seemed to melt. She was just like our mother in this way: summer was a problem for Mama, too. We had to bring her up to the mountains where, in the cooler air, she would instantly feel fine again."

The bishop counseled prudence. Gianna was a good woman, well prepared scientifically, healthy, and athletic. But perhaps these were not the only prerequisites for undertaking so difficult a life. He concluded, "When the Lord calls a worker into his vineyard, he prepares that worker for the task

Gianna skiing on the slopes of Sestriére, Italy (1953)

and provides for everything. I don't know whether this is your sister's authentic vocation. So many obstacles stand in the way...."

Father Giuseppe relayed Bishop Bernareggi's advice to Gianna. And it seemed to her to be an authoritative call for deeper reflection on the matter.

However, in 1952, she wrote to Father Alberto:

> I am still waiting to know exactly when I should come. Cecco says that I could go back with him. Nando and Zita say that I could help you greatly by staying there to work. The bishop should send me his request, otherwise how will I arrange all the papers? Write to me soon.

Father Alberto's response was prompt. He advised Gianna to weigh carefully what she considered doing and to postpone any decision until it was possible to talk to him directly. He described the situation of his mission very realistically, and then counseled:

> If this letter reaches you too late, that is, if you have already said yes to someone or to something, *do me the favor of telling them that you still have not decided anything for certain.* At least wait a while, because I want to talk to you about this matter....
>
> You have always expressed your willingness to come as soon as the bishop would send you, thus confirming your intention to spend your life helping the poor. I had written you once that if the Lord called you to family life...you would be offered the opportunity to give the Church a priest, for whom Brazil has extreme need. But, if forming a family is not your path, why not come here where you

> could practically take the place of a priest by your work as a physician and your involvement in Catholic Action?

Essentially, her brother was advising Gianna to discern whether the missions were her true call from God and to remind her that marriage was another, equally important vocation.

Meanwhile, the young doctor continued to worry about the medical care of the women of Grajau. If she could not go herself, then she would try to find another doctor to assist her brother in the specific field of obstetrics and gynecology. Among Gianna's documents are the rough drafts of two letters sent to Dr. Marcello Candia and Professor Canova, both well known for their commitment to aiding the poor in northern Brazil.

Gianna continued her work while discerning her vocation. She asked for God to enlighten her with regard to his will. Toward the end of 1952, she sent a letter to Father Alberto:

> I am writing to tell you that I want to think things over carefully and to pray. All in all, it would be better to wait a few more years. You advised me not to make any commitments to the Prelature and to come for a tour. If this precaution is because of the climate, I could adapt to it just as you have, but I think it would be fairer and safer for me to come down when you have things arranged. Then there is also the matter [of my practice in Mesero], which I don't really know how I will resolve.

While this exchange of correspondence between Magenta and Brazil continued, Gianna was passionately involved in the daily care of her patients. She participated enthusiastically in the life of Catholic Action and the Society of St. Vincent de Paul—the two pillars on which she based her active Christian life. Her dream of journeying to mission lands returned from time to time, but it was to remain unrealized. Nevertheless, she believed it was important "to be of service, to take care of daily matters well," as Sister Virginia recalls, "even the most insignificant or less satisfying matters; doing them well and, above all, willingly by abandoning herself to God's providence."

9

To Be Helpful and Not Judgmental

Although the search for her place in the world sometimes drew her into moments of melancholy, Gianna was essentially a happy person. Throughout her life, she had felt loved and understood. Her youth had been filled with affection from her family and the serene years she had spent within the religious atmosphere of her home had shaped in her a personality of unshakeable certainties and remarkable inner strength. Gianna received her education in good schools and learned from competent teachers; she enjoyed the privilege of being able to choose a medical profession—unusual for a woman at the time—without fear of opposition from her family.

Gianna's home life taught her to pass on the fruits of the love she received to those who were less fortunate. Whatever she received, she shared generously. With profound awareness of her responsibility to share, she gave herself entirely to her work.

Gianna had begun her practice as soon as she became a member of the Physicians' Professional Board for Milan and the Province. In July 1950, she became a member of the Mutual Association of Physicians and practiced until just a few days before her death. Neither her marriage nor the birth of her children distracted her from her service to the sick. In those days, perhaps this kind of self-giving aroused the curiosity in the residents of Mesero and Magenta. After all, why should a married woman pursue such a demanding profession, however worthy? Gianna considered her work her mission, and Gianna's patients responded to her care and devotion with an equal love and trust. Gianna especially loved working among the poor, the elderly, mothers, and children; with them, she was able to put into practice her ideal of the "Christian physician" who touches "Jesus in the bodies of the sick."

During the summer of 1952, she served as a pediatrician at the parish summer camp in Ameno, a little village on Lake Orta. The following year, she accompanied a group of ailing people to Lourdes. Deeply moved by this splendid human and spiritual experience, she enrolled in the Association of Catholic Physicians and then in the International Medical Association of Our Lady of Lourdes in 1954. After her wedding in September of 1955, she took on even more responsibilities. Besides her regular practice in Mesero and her house calls to the rich and poor, she became the director of the nursery at the Onmi Clinic of Ponte Nuovo of Magenta and volunteered at the nursery school of the small village that had become her home.

Gianna's patients have many lively memories of her that reveal her love and devotion to her mission. Her attention to

Dr. Gianna Beretta, 1951

every individual, combined with her professional attitude, inspired confidence. No one had to plead with Gianna to make a house call, even at night; she refused no one. She felt special tenderness for mothers and elderly women, who sometimes paid her with a few fresh eggs, or a chicken, or a bouquet of wild flowers. Some of Gianna's patients remember how, knowing their economic circumstances, she would often leave behind some money and medicine after a house call.

She would have long discussions with mothers not only about the best way to raise their children, but also about the absolute value of life. She suffered deeply whenever she met a woman who wanted to have an abortion. "It is a sin against God," she would plead. "Life is sacred."

Gianna specialized in pediatrics because she loved children and because she desired to have continual contact with mothers through them. Many of the mothers she encountered were young women like her. Their problems often placed them in serious situations. Her feminine perspective allowed Gianna to empathize with their struggles and sorrows. As she came to know them better, she could plant a seed of hope and trust in life, and guide them toward embracing the will of God.

While she was still attending medical school, Gianna wrote that she would make every effort "not to judge" those she encountered. Gianna understood that the benefits she had received in her life—growing up in an atmosphere of deep faith—was not everyone's experience. Now, her work as a doctor put her in a position to practice her earlier resolution.

No one who met Gianna experienced any trace of intolerance or condemnation, because she strove to make her actions consistent with her beliefs. There must have been difficult moments for her, since she worked among the people and shared in their affairs—both good and bad. She did not concern herself only with a patient's physical well being, but she was always as interested in their personal situations.

In Gianna's day, as is so frequently the case today, many women turned to abortion to deal with an unwanted pregnancy. Gianna profoundly believed in the sacred value of every human life. No matter what the scenario, when a choice had to be made she did not hesitate to choose life, so deep was her conviction. Yet, despite her firm beliefs, she never presumed to set herself up as a judge of those women who did not have the same principles or determination.

When her patients considered the possibility of an abortion, Gianna suffered tremendously. While consistently defending the right to life of every human being from the first moment of its conception and trying to help women to understand the sanctity of life, she never turned her back on them as they struggled.

Gianna was maternal toward those who were struggling personally with this issue. Once, a young woman asked Gianna to come to her home because of some "mysterious" hemorrhaging, which was actually the result of an attempted abortion. Gianna treated her compassionately, but firmly, urging her to seriously consider what she had done.

On another occasion, Gianna treated a young woman who had had an abortion. With particular kindness, Gianna offered the young woman some words on the sacredness of human life, which the patient listened to attentively. Gianna gently encouraged the woman to face the seriousness of her act and to realize that what she had done was not only an offense against her child, but also against God. Gianna invited her patient to be reconciled with the Lord, and she encouraged her to embrace God's infinite mercy.

Gianna brought comfort to everyone she met. The examples are many. For instance, she spared no effort to help the family of a boy who was born with a serious cervical hernia. She consulted specialists and convinced the desperate parents to permit their child to undergo the operation that would save his life. Or again, there was one woman who, long after her other children had already grown, realized she was pregnant. She felt a kind of shame and discomfort in the presence of anyone she knew. Gianna's love of nature in all its expressions helped to encourage this woman—and all her patients—to welcome the joy of motherhood, whatever its circumstances.

As a physician, she cared for her littlest patients with the same love she had for her own children. She preferred to deliver babies at home; in her day, hospitals or clinics were necessary only in cases when a mother or infant were at risk. She felt that welcoming a new life within the home was an act of thanksgiving for God's blessings on the family. Gianna passionately believed that a new baby was always a priceless gift. She would even encourage her pastor to speak about the necessity of defending innocent life in his sermons.

Gianna's days were full; she lived and worked among people she could help and love. Every day she thanked God for giving her the grace to be involved in a profession that allowed her to realize her ideals of service and apostolate. This was a peaceful and happy period in her life and she did not seem troubled by questions about her future.

It was about this time in her life that Gianna wrote some of her thoughts on the value of a single smile, which her husband would later call her "true hymn to joy."

Smile at God, from whom every gift comes to us;
smile at the Father with ever more perfect prayer;
smile at the Holy Spirit;
smile at Jesus who you approach at Mass, in Holy Communion, and in Eucharistic adoration;
smile at the person who represents Christ on earth: the Pope;
smile at your confessor, the one who personifies God even when he challenges you to reject sin;
smile at the Blessed Virgin, to whose example you must conform your life, so that, seeing you, people might be led to holy thoughts;
smile at your Guardian Angel, because this angel has been given to you by God to lead you into Paradise;
smile at your parents, brothers, and sisters, even when they challenge your pride;
smile always in forgiving offenses;
smile in associating with others, banishing all criticism and murmuring;
Smile at everyone the Lord sends you during the day.

The world seeks joy, but cannot find it far from God. We must understand that our joy comes from Jesus.

With Jesus in our hearts, we bear joy—he is the strength that helps us.

Happiness is having Jesus in our hearts.

But the secret of happiness is to live moment by moment, and to thank the Lord for everything he sends us out of his goodness. *

**From a letter written to Pietro Molla just a few days before their wedding.*

10

Discovering Love: Pietro Molla

At age thirty-two, Gianna led a tranquil and fulfilled life. Every day, she drove to Colombaia Square in Mesero to open her office and begin seeing the growing number of patients who came to her. The people of the surrounding area were quite pleased with "their doctor" and willingly accepted her treatment and advice.

The Molla family lived in the building that faced Gianna's office, and they followed the young doctor's activities with interest. Their son, Pietro, was the joy and pride of the Mollas. He was an engineer who held the position of technical vice-director of La Saffa, a company that drove the economy of the whole region at that time.

Pietro Molla scarcely knew the doctor who welcomed long lines of patients to her office every day. He met her once at her office while waiting for an appointment with Ferdinando for a minor ailment. Then, on another occasion, Pietro met Gianna at the hospital where she was treating his sister Teresina, who was seriously ill. These were fleeting encounters, but Pietro Molla did not forget them. From the very first, Gianna seemed to be a very special woman to Pietro, who characterized her as "genuine and serious."

When Gianna hired a nurse for her practice, their casual encounters became more frequent. The nurse was Luigina Garavaglia, who happened to reside across the street from Gianna's office—in the Molla home. Pietro would see Gianna when she and Luigina met at the Mollas to discuss the next day's work. Pietro drove by Gianna in the morning on the way to work, and in the evening Pietro watched as Gianna left her office.

Pietro's admiration for Gianna continued to grow. He began to realize that the beautiful, trim woman in the white coat—who everyone respected and loved—enchanted him. Yet, he had not had the opportunity to spend any time with her beyond their occasional brief greetings and quick smiles. Then an opportunity presented itself. Father Lino, a mutual friend from Mesero, invited them both to his first Mass.

Pietro described the joy of this night in a diary entry:

> I remember you as you congratulated Father Lino and his family with your gentle, kind smile. I think of how devoutly you made the sign of the cross before the meal. I can see you in prayer at the Eucharistic benediction. I still feel your cordial handshake and I see again the sweet and bright smile that accompanied it.

The next day, as if to solidify the initial sensation of love, he again wrote in his diary: "I sense a tranquility that makes me feel certain of having made a good impression. The Immaculate Mother has blessed me!"

The engaged couple in Livrio (1955)

Gianna had come back from her pilgrimage to Lourdes just a few months before Father Lino's Mass. Before leaving Lourdes, she had prayed for the Virgin Mary's help to see her vocation clearly. Gianna believed her meeting Pietro that night was the beginning of a response to her prayer.

The two young people began to cross paths more often, and to feel that they were becoming very important to each other. Then, they celebrated New Year's Eve together at La Scala—the opera house in Milan. After the performance, Pietro was welcomed into the Beretta home for the first time, where he toasted the New Year with Gianna and her family. His diary reveals the love that was maturing in his heart: "This evening represents a decisive moment in my dreams for my future. I entrust myself to Our Lady of Good Counsel."

After that "decisive" evening, Gianna and Pietro saw each other more and more frequently. They confided in one another, talked about their hopes and desires, and came to understand each other more deeply. They had so many things in common: their fundamental certainties and the great hopes that gave meaning to their lives. They were truly happy together.

Gianna's first letter to Pietro, dated February 21, 1955, was a response to his proposal of marriage. She confided her desire to attain with him "a level of trust that will allow us to understand one another more and more and to love each other always." Then she joyfully accepted his proposal and concluded her letter with these words:

> I want to make you happy and be what you desire: kind, understanding, and ready for the sacrifices that life will require. I haven't told you yet that I have always been very

sensitive and eager for affection. While I had my parents, their love was enough for me. Then, although remaining very united to the Lord and working for him, I felt the need for a mother and I found her in the dear nun I told you about yesterday. Now you are here whom I love, and I intend to give myself to you, to form a truly Christian family. Ciao, dear Pietro....

Pietro's response to Gianna's letter is a splendid testimony to their growing love:

My dearest Gianna,

I have read your letter many times and I have kissed it. A new life is beginning for me: a life with your great affection and luminous kindness. We are beginning a life of love together.

I love you, my sweet Gianna. The Mother of Heaven, Our Lady of Good Counsel, to whom I have prayed in our little church of Ponte Nuovo, could not have given me a greater or more desirable grace.

I have so great a need and desire for affection and for a family of my own. Now I have you, your love and your gift, and I am happy. My heart is yours and I want to form my family with you. I too want to make you happy and to understand you fully.

The couple joyfully explored their mutual love. On March 7, 1955, Pietro wrote in his diary: "The more I know Gianna, the more I am convinced that God could not have given me a greater gift than her love and companionship."

That month, Gianna decided to go skiing with her sister Zita and a friend at Sestriére. She loved the sensation of flying down the long slopes of the still-snowy mountains in early spring. After this vacation, Gianna returned to Magenta and resumed her practice with renewed energy. Pietro, falling more deeply in love, gave her a stunning diamond ring. Touched, Gianna sent him a very tender letter:

My dearest Pietro,

How can I thank you for the magnificent ring? Pietro dear, in exchange I give you my heart and I will always love you as I love you now. You are the dearest person to me, and my thoughts, affections, and desires are continually turning toward you on this eve of our engagement. I can't wait for the moment when I can be yours forever. Pietro dearest, you know that I want to see you and to know that you are happy; tell me what I should be and what I should do to make you so. I have great trust in the Lord, and I am certain that he will help me to become your worthy spouse.

I often meditate on the text [associated with] Saint Anne: "A strong woman, who will find her? The heart of her husband can trust in her. She will do only good things for him and never bring evil upon him throughout all of his life."

Pietro, I want to be that strong woman for you! Instead, I feel weak. This means that I must lean on your strong arm. I feel so safe, so close to you! I ask you a favor: from now on, Pietro, if you see me doing something wrong...tell me, okay?

Gianna and Pietro celebrated the official announcement of their engagement within the intimacy of their families on April 11, the day after Easter. Gianna gave Pietro a gold watch, which he still keeps with him. Three days later, Gianna received a long letter from Pietro.

A photo of Gianna that was taken by her fiancé Pietro Molla, during a trip to the lake at Como

My dearest Gianna,

I am still living in the great joy of our engagement and in the sweetest happiness that is renewed every moment that I am aware that your "thoughts, affections, and desires" are turned to me. I want this sweetest joy to be yours, too, the fair object of my "thoughts, of all my affection, of my desires." The gift of your heart and your love have found my heart to be all yours and my love will be only and always for you, O my dearest Gianna.

You are my jewel, the fairest, and so sweetly dear in virtue and goodness, in beauty and in your smile. More intense than the reflection of light from your engagement ring is what I want my love for you to be.

The beautiful watch you gave me accompanies me through the most beautiful time of my life: the time of our love and our family. You are the strong woman whom I have sought from heaven, and whom the heavenly Mother has given to me.

I will entrust my heart to you always and I will receive every good thing from you.

Love me always as you love me now. Always be as affectionate and kind, caring, sweet, and understanding to me as you are now. See how you are making me happy now, and how I urge you to do so always!

You *are* the strong woman of the Bible for me.

At your side, my joy is perfect. Surely, you will give me no occasion to have to mention any faults. To your request, I respond with the same request in my regard. I still see you, so devout at our engagement Mass, and I feel certain of the Divine blessings warmly invoked by dear Father Giuseppe.

« 11 »

Physician, Wife, Mother

The months passed quickly. Gianna continued to serve her patients and work among the young girls of Catholic Action. Always smiling and active, she was busy with the many details involved in preparing for her wedding. Gianna exchanged advice and confidences with her best friend Mariuccia Parmeggiani, who was preparing for her own wedding. Mariuccia remembers this as "...a beautiful time—we were so happy."

Pietro and Gianna bought furniture for their home and happily planned their new life together. Gianna looked eagerly to her future, having no doubts now about her place in the world. She was certain that marrying Pietro was indeed her vocation.

Gianna's personal notes provide some insight into her ideas on vocation:

> Everything has a specific end; everything obeys a law. God has shown each one of us the way, the vocation, and the life of grace that lies beyond physical life. Our earthly and eternal happiness depends on following our vocation without

> faltering. What is a vocation? It is a gift from God—it comes from God himself! Our concern, then, should be to know the will of God. We should enter onto the path that God wills for us, not by "forcing the door," but when God wills and as God wills....

During the last months of their engagement, Pietro was often away on brief business trips. The longest one, from September 3 to 11, took Pietro to Denmark and Sweden. During those nine days of separation, the couple stayed close through the many letters they wrote to each other. They experienced a spiritual "togetherness" despite the many miles that lay between them.

Pietro returned home and on the night before their wedding he gave Gianna a gold watch and a pearl necklace along with this love note:

> Gianna, let these crown the wonder and the brightness of your beauty and your virtues on our wedding day. May the watch always mark the loveliest and most peaceful times of our life, and may this pearl necklace be a sign of the enchanting light of our love. They are given to you, with great affection, by your mother and my mother, and by your Pietro with the greatest love.

September 24, 1955 dawned a beautiful, cloudless day. Filled with emotion, Pietro waited at the altar in the Basilica of San Martino in Magenta where everything was adorned with white and pink carnations, and the long carpet extending the length of the church was lined with flowers and greenery. Father Giuseppe, standing near Pietro, had the joy of performing the ceremony. Gianna arrived dressed in a white

The joyful bride in the garden outside her home in Magenta, September 1955

satin gown and a tulle veil pinned at the nape of her neck. Happiness radiated in her smiling face and glowing eyes. The moment she appeared on Ferdinando's arm at the door of the basilica, the crowd in the church broke into loud applause while the bells rang on joyously.

Gianna and Pietro knelt together and promised to remain united to each other forever with the words of the vows of the Sacrament of Matrimony—to live their life together and to love each other "for better or worse." "So often," Pietro Molla later wrote Gianna, "the memory returns of that sudden outburst of applause that began upon your entrance into the church that lasted until you reached the altar. Your brother Giuseppe, who blessed our union, exhorted us to give witness to the Gospel and to holiness."

After the reception in the garden of the Beretta home, the couple left for a long honeymoon in southern Italy. After their stop in Rome, they traveled to Naples, Ischia, Capri, and then Palermo, Syracuse, Catania and, finally, Taormina, where they stayed at the "San Domenico," an old monastery converted into a beautiful inn.

Pietro and Gianna took a plane back to Milan and immediately left for Germany and Holland by train. Pietro had important appointments in Düsseldorf, Cologne, Hanover, and Amsterdam. It was another new and happy experience for the new bride to share in the responsibilities of Pietro's professional life.

Upon their return, the newlyweds began their life together. They made their home in a lovely villa, the traditional

Gianna poses for a photo during her honeymoon

residence of the factory manager, on La Saffa's property in Ponte Nuovo near Mesero.

Gianna resumed work immediately. Anyone who needed her found her available at any hour. And Pietro faithfully accompanied Gianna to her patients' homes when they called at night.

The Mollas' home, furnished with wedding gifts and articles Pietro and Gianna brought from their previous homes, began to take on more and more of Gianna's loving touch. The result was a home that somehow reflected her personality and character: cheerful paintings on the walls, a photograph of their wedding in a silver frame, their most treasured books.

Every day, she stopped in the nearby parish church to pray before the Holy Eucharist. The pastor, Father Agostino Cerri, remembers Gianna as "a serene woman, filled with a joy that seemed to spread out to all who were near her."

Because of increased managerial responsibilities, Pietro would leave every morning at 8:00 A.M. and return home very late in the evening. His work often took him away, but Gianna knew that Pietro, like herself—though in a very different field—was at the service of others.

Only one small cloud hung over their lives: their hope of having a child was not immediately fulfilled. Gianna confided her worries to Virginia: "Unfortunately," she wrote, "I do not feel any signs of pregnancy. Pray that the Lord will soon send me many fine and healthy children."

Gianna did not have to wait much longer for this blessing. Just over a year after their marriage, Pietro and Gianna joyfully welcomed their first son into the world on November 19, 1956. Pierluigi was born in their Ponte Nuovo home and, a few days later, baptized there by his Uncle Giuseppe. The little boy's arrival was the crowning of the couple's dreams: they now felt themselves a "real" family.

Gianna quickly returned to her active life with the help of Savina Passeri, a young woman who became the Mollas' housekeeper and was devoted to Gianna, remaining with the family until after the "signora's" death.

In addition to the usual responsibilities of her practice, Gianna agreed to become the primary physician for the children of the Onmi Nursery and the elementary school in Ponte Nuovo. She took good care of the children, gently banishing their fears with her kindness while easing their pains.

Mother Emma Ciserani, the Canossian Sister in charge of the Omni Nursery, recalls how Gianna "was always ready to help and treated every child with the delicacy possessed by one who sees the image of Jesus in every human being. She leaned over each child with a gentle and genuine interest. I often heard mothers praising her as they dropped their children off in the morning. I know that she always ran out at night for every call without letting her tiredness affect her services."

That summer, Gianna spent a few months in a small rented house in the mountains at Courmayeur. The air, pure and cool, was good for her and for the baby. Pietro spent much of his time with his two "treasures." Carrying Pierluigi on his back, he and Gianna would take long, peaceful walks on the mountainside.

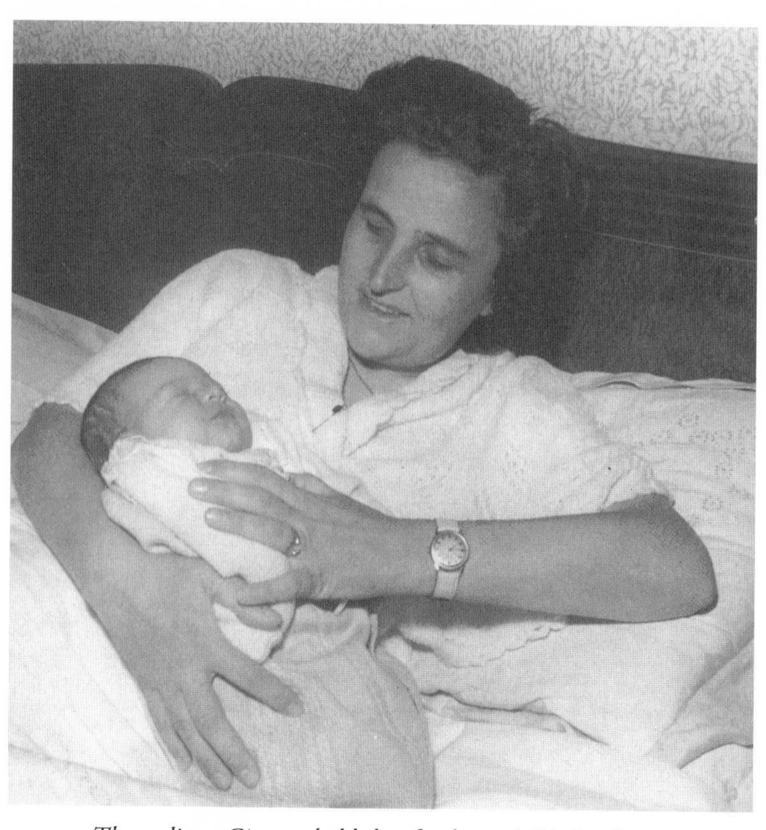

The radiant Gianna holds her firstborn child, Pierluigi, in their home at Ponte Nuovo, November 19, 1956

Gianna with Pierluigi enjoying the beauty of Courmayeur during the summer of 1957

Pietro, Gianna, and Pierluigi during the summer of 1957

Gianna, Pietro, and Pierluigi on vacation at Courmayeur

A formal portrait of Gianna and Pierluigi, on his first birthday

Before long, the family had reason for greater happiness. Gianna was expecting her second child. On December 11, 1957, little Maria Zita was born in the Ponte Nuovo home. As with Pierluigi's birth, Ferdinando was there to assist Gianna. Father Giuseppe baptized Maria Zita, affectionately called Mariolina, just a few days later in the parish church.

As the months passed, Gianna and Pietro began to experience the stress of their increased duties and responsibilities. Gianna cared for the children while continuing her medical practice but Pietro, burdened with the concerns and responsibilities of his own work, needed a retreat from daily pressures. He spent some time alone in Sanremo.

Gianna sadly watched him leave. She knew it was important for him to rest in order to be able to deal with his difficult tasks at La Saffa, so she chose to accept his absence and decided not to worry him with any family matters while he was away. And there *were* things that concerned her as a parent: Pierluigi was not doing well at the time, and Mariolina was restless at night. Gianna began to feel very tired; yet, with her characteristic love and patience, she did her utmost to care for and soothe her children by herself until Pietro returned.

On February 26, Gianna wrote to Pietro, saying that she was eager for his return. She missed his warm embrace and the strength and support of his presence. Despite his absence, Gianna believed that Pietro not only loved her tenderly, but also understood her and completed her as a human being. Her love for Pietro continued to grow stronger; in fact, he seemed indispensable to her. In the deepest, most religious

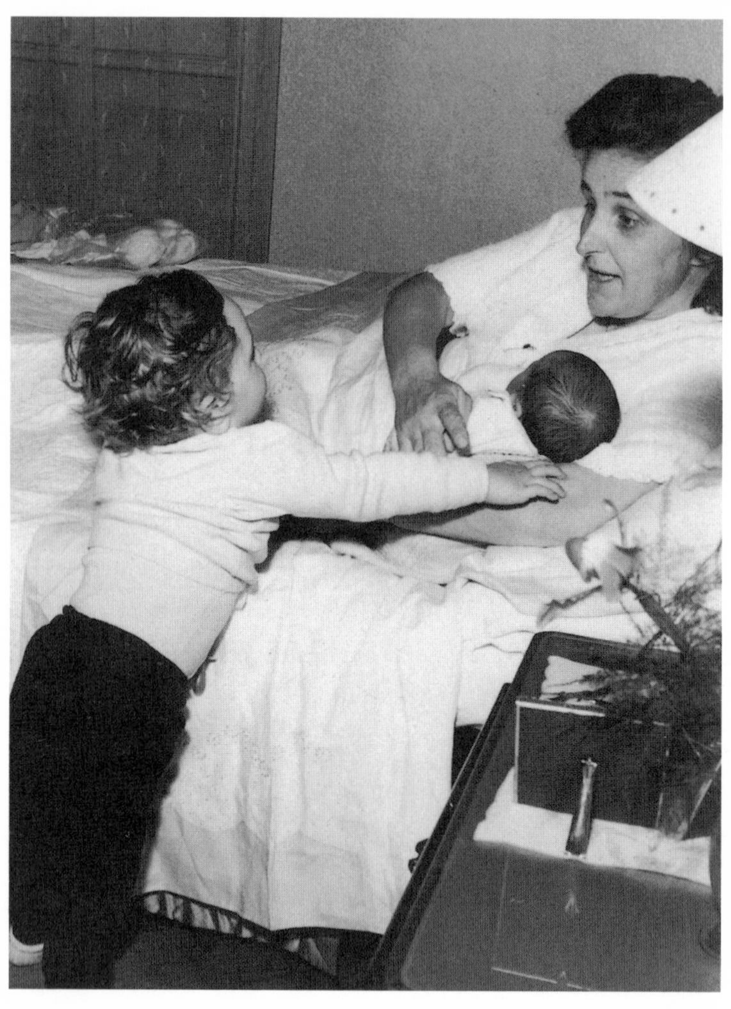

Gianna showing the curious Pierluigi his newborn sister, Mariolina

sense, her love was complete; Gianna felt that her love for Pietro was connected to her love for God.

In spite of their busy schedules, Gianna and Pietro went to Milan regularly to spend time together at concerts or plays or movies. The children were well looked after and loved by Savina, Aunt Zita, and their paternal grandmother who occasionally stayed with them for a few hours. Gianna's two small children always held first place in her heart and she showered affection and care on them both, but especially on Mariolina, who suffered from some bone problems and had to wear a brace.

In the summer of 1958, Gianna left her office in the hands of her brother Ferdinando, closed the Ponte Nuovo house, and set out for the mountains with her little family. Pietro spent the entire vacation with them, and life moved on with a pleasantly regular rhythm.

The Berettas and the Mollas celebrated that Christmas together. Gianna felt a tender happiness and gratitude for the third child she was now expecting. The Lord had been kind to her; she had dreamed of raising a family founded on good Christian principles and the love of God. Her greatest desire was for her children to flourish "like olive shoots around her table" (cf. Psalm 28). Her dreams were becoming a marvelous reality.

With all the new blessings in her life, Gianna never lost touch with her brothers and sisters. Even after her marriage, the tight bond of friendship that always united them was not broken. Gianna corresponded frequently with her siblings who were far from home: Sister Virginia, who was still working among the poor of India, and Father Alberto, who continued to live and work among the *campesinos* in Brazil. Gianna wrote to them about her life's daily events and always wanted to know about theirs.

12
Anxious Moments

In the spring of 1959, from April 26 to June 17, Pietro had to make a very long business trip to the United States. Gianna was expecting her third child.

It was a stressful time for Gianna. She was anxious about her pregnancy, which was a difficult one. As usual, she was very busy with her work as well as with Pierluigi and Mariolina who were still very young and required a lot of attention. This, and the heaviness of Pietro's absence, must have contributed to her physical exhaustion.

Intellectually, she fully understood the reasons for Pietro's absence, but she could not help wanting him to be home at such an important time. She also worried something might happen to Pietro. He worked extremely hard and was under such constant stress that she feared for his health. Gianna was concerned about his frequent international flights and the possible dangers that might accompany them.

Gianna tried to be strong for Pietro. In her letters, which she wrote regularly (thirty-one on this trip), she tried to sound serene in order to ease his mind about her and the children, and also to prevent the burden of the distance between them from weighing on him.* While Pietro was in the U.S., she sometimes confided in Mariuccia, and yet also tried to conceal problems even from her. This letter, written immediately after her husband's return to Ponte Nuovo, reveals how difficult this must have been.

> A month ago, I had to be rushed to the hospital because of toxemia. I had terrible pains, continuous contractions, fever, and vomiting. I ran the risk of losing the baby. Thoroughly frightened, I obeyed Nando and let myself be brought to Monza. It was midnight, and an obstetrician I know well was waiting for me. With oxygen, sedatives, and hypodermics, the crisis passed. Two days later, I was able to go to Malpensa Airport to meet Pietro who, unaware of what had happened, was returning from the United States.

On July 15, less than a month after Pietro's return, Laura made her entrance into the loving circle of the Molla family as its newest member.

"Gianna could have given me no greater gift so soon after my return from America," Pietro told me. Gianna's love and the thought of his children accompanied him in his travels and kept him spiritually united to his wife and family during the long days of separation.

**Seventy-three survive and are collected in* Love Letters to My Husband: Blessed Gianna Beretta Molla *(Boston: Pauline Books & Media, 2002).*

The adoring Gianna with Pierluigi and Mariolina during a trip to Ponte Nuovo (1959)

Gianna feeding Mariolina under Pierluigi's watchful eye during an outing (1958)

"On July 31," Pietro recalled, "we went up to Verrand, in Courmayeur, to a little villa in the meadows. It was a beautiful, remote area, not full of construction as it is now. Pierluigi and Mariolina had already been there for several days, and Gianna and I joined them, carrying newborn Laura with us. We spent unforgettable days there together. I was able to stay with them for the whole month of August. Gianna returned home with the children at the end of September. They were doing very well and the mountain air seemed to have suited them."

After returning to Ponte Nuovo, Gianna tried to reorganize her life, wanting to find time for everything: Pietro and her children, the management of her household, and her medical practice. Pietro saw how busy she always was and asked if she would consider giving up her practice. The look Gianna gave him in response, however, discouraged Pietro from asking again.

"I promise you," she told him one day, "that when we have one more child, I will stop my medical work and will be a full-time mother, even though that will be difficult for me."

Gianna was approaching forty and she dreamed of having another baby. "We are getting old," she would joke now and then, "and we have to do something soon...."

Coming from a large family, Gianna had always wanted to have at least four children and to watch them grow up together, healthy and happy.

Gianna with Pierluigi and Mariolina
in their garden at Ponte Nuovo

≺ 13 ≻

Tensions and Hopes

Between their rapidly growing children and their daily concerns, the year 1960 passed quickly for Gianna and Pietro. In the summer, the entire family went to Courmayeur for vacation. Once again, they experienced the joy of time together as a family that loved each other very much.

In December, Pietro had to go on another business trip, but this time he wanted Gianna to join him. Entrusting their children to Aunt Zita and Savina, Gianna and Pietro went first to England, and then to Holland. They treasured being together, seeing new places and meeting new people, and Gianna enjoyed the unanticipated time alone with her husband.

And, always a mother, Gianna called home every day for all the news about Pierluigi, Mariolina, and Lauretta.

In July 1961, Gianna accompanied Pietro on a business trip to Denmark and Sweden—countries she had already heard much about through the long letters Pietro had written before their wedding. Now she looked forward to visiting these places, which had so intrigued her, with Pietro.

Gianna poses for a photo in Stockholm, where she accompanied Pietro on one of his business trips (July 1961)

After they returned to Italy, Gianna took the children to Courmayeur together with Mariuccia and her children—her dearest friend having finally accepted Gianna's long-standing invitation to spend their vacation together.

Mariuccia clearly recalls the enthusiasm and joy of those summer days. The two women and their cheerful tribe formed one large family, determined to enjoy the beauty of the mountains. The two friends spent hours discussing their children and their plans for the future. Gianna took long walks in the woods to be refreshed by the mountain air. Before long, Pietro also joined them in their mountain retreat.

And then, Gianna realized she was expecting her fourth child. Pietro and Gianna rejoiced that their desire for another child would be fulfilled, and they thanked God for yet another blessing.

During the happy weeks that followed, Gianna's pregnancy seemed to progress normally until she began to notice an abnormal swelling in her abdomen. Something was wrong; she and Pietro decided to return to Magenta immediately.

Leaving the children in the care of Mariuccia and Savina, Gianna calmly returned home. She did not feel excessively worried—she knew she would be in the good hands of her brother Ferdinando, and she hoped to be able to return to her family within a few days.

Ferdinando remembers well those difficult days:

> In examining my sister, I discovered a large tumor growing alongside the uterus, which was beginning to cause her a great deal of pain. I had her go to Dr. Mario Vitali for an emergency examination. He confirmed my diagnosis and

Pietro, Gianna, Pierluigi, Mariolina, and Lauretta relaxing on their family vacation in Courmayeur, 1960

> advised immediate surgery, believing a clearer judgment on the situation could be made during the procedure. Since Gianna was a doctor, all the risks to her and the baby she had carried for little more than two months were clear.

This began the truly heroic period of Gianna Beretta Molla's life. "I remember discussing the situation at length with Gianna," recalls Ferdinando. "She listened to me patiently and attentively, but showed one decisive concern: that her baby be saved. And this was the desire that she expressed to Dr. Vitali when she underwent the surgery a few days later."

Before undergoing surgery, Gianna wrote to Mariuccia:

> Finally, I will tell you what happened to me. On Tuesday, when Nando examined me, he found that there was a rather large growth near my uterus. We thought it might be an ovarian cyst. I went to Dr. Vitali and he confirmed our suspicions and said that it would be better to remove it within the next two weeks. I had already decided to return to Courmayeur the next day, but I began hemorrhaging in the morning. Right away to bed, injections, ice packs, etc., and so the hemorrhaging stopped. Since vomiting persists, the doctor also thinks that perhaps it was just a threat of a miscarriage and that the pregnancy is continuing. They have decided it is better to do surgery right away, so it will be next week.
>
> Dear Mariuccia, you can imagine what I have been experiencing, how my heart and thoughts turn toward my dearest treasures. I trust in the Lord and in Our Lady of Healing. Have my little ones pray—Our Lady always hears the prayers of the innocent.

To Savina, many, many greetings and thanks for what she is doing for the children. To you, Mariuccia, the most affectionate kisses and heartfelt thanks. To my treasures and to your little ones, big, big kisses.

The surgery took place on September 6, 1961. Ferdinando assisted Dr. Stradella in the operating room. It was Ferdinando who wrote the clinical report, which reads:

After two months of gestation, a painful symptomatology occurred of a spontaneous, abortion-inducing type, with light metrorrhagia [profuse uterine bleeding] immediately controlled by antihemorrhagics and uterine sedatives. Since a miscarriage did not occur and the painful symptomatology continued to increase, the gynecological surgeon decided on a laparotomy.

Before surgery, in the presence of Dr. Vitali, the husband, and the undersigned, the patient did not hesitate to place the baby's life ahead of her own, knowing what could occur, and pleaded with the surgeon to respect her wishes during the operation.

Upon opening the abdominal cavity, the surgeon discovered a large mass of serous uterine tumor situated between the uterine posterior wall and the right lateral, in the intramural part and in the subserous part. With skillful hands the surgeon removed the large neoplastic mass, performing correct hemostasis, without injuring the uterine cavity, carefully suturing the edges of the surgical wound so as to allow the pregnancy to continue, contrary to the normal practice of total destruction, otherwise justified, for avoiding further and serious risks to the mother. A suture performed on the uterus in the early months of pregnancy often gives way to a secondary rupture of the uterus and to immediate lethal danger to the patient in the fourth or fifth month of gestation, a fact well-known to Dr. Gianna Beretta Molla.

Concerned for the well being of the pregnant patient, we watched for the signs of a spontaneous miscarriage in the post-operative period; there was indeed a threat of miscarriage for about three weeks....

A week after the operation, Gianna wrote to Mariuccia again:

My dearest Mariuccia, today they removed the stitches, so I can answer your dear letter. Infinite thanks for what you are still doing for my treasures and I am sure they have found an affectionate and kind second mother in you. I am only afraid—and this would make me so unhappy—that you are tiring yourself too much.

Pietro has told me that your little ones are beginning to feel the advantage of the air in Courmayeur and I am very glad that they have good appetites.

I hope that Gian Piero [Mariuccia's husband] can also go for some days to keep you company and to enjoy his little family....

The doctor has not said when he will release me. Everything went fine with the operation, but he still fears a miscarriage and wants me to stay for a few days. As soon as he tells me, I will let you know. However, a trip to Courmayeur would be imprudent even though everything has gone well so far.

Dear Mariuccia, be happy, and we will soon be able to see each other. Big kisses to all our beautiful little ones and a big hug to you.

Gianna enjoying the outdoors with Mariolina and Lauretta at Courmayeur (1960)

In her letter to Mariuccia, Gianna added some words for her children:

> My dearest treasures, Papa is going to bring you many big kisses; I wish so much that I could come too, but I have to stay in bed because I have a little tummy ache. Be good children and do what Mariuccia and Savina tell you. Pierluigi, you are the oldest, so help your little sisters play without fighting. Mariolina, you are the older sister, so be kind and nice to Lauretta.
>
> I hold you all here in my heart and I am thinking about you every minute. Say a Hail Mary for me, so that Our Lady will help me get better quickly, and then I can come back to Courmayeur and hug you all and stay with you always. Your Mama kisses and hugs each of you with much affection.

Gianna also wrote to Father Alberto from the hospital: "Dear Father Alberto, I am getting better every day. I truly hope that the Madonna will help me to carry this pregnancy to term."

And to Zita: "If it's a boy, we will call him Enrico, and perhaps he will become Father Enrico!"

Gianna confessed impulsively to a visiting friend, "I've suffered a lot, but I am happy because the pregnancy is saved. I'm hoping for a boy!"

The Molla children came back from Courmayeur while Gianna was still in the hospital. When the doctors finally discharged her, she returned home. She recuperated gradually, and before long was able to resume her life and work. She went to her office every day and frequently loaded her children into her car to drop them off in Magenta where Zita cared for them. The children loved their aunt who was so patient and affectionate. In the warm autumn sun of Lombardy, it was lovely to play in their grandparent's large garden, to run among the rows of grapes in the vineyard, and to gather late flowers to give to their Mama.

While everything seemed to be back to normal, Gianna knew full well the consequences of her decision, that is, the danger to her life if a second uterine rupture occurred, but she did not seem worried. With unconquerable hope in God's help, Gianna continued her day-to-day life.

« 14 »

The Birth of Gianna Emanuela

It was a rainy day in Lombardy when I visited Mariuccia's lovely home in Besnate Ticino to speak with her about Gianna and their close relationship. We paged through some photo albums together, looking at the happy faces of the children—hers and Gianna's—when they were small and played together.

Both women being pregnant at the same time had seemed to draw them even closer together. But as close as their friendship had become, Mariuccia never suspected Gianna might have been in any danger. During the seven long months after her operation, no one noticed any change in Gianna, not even Mariuccia who continued to receive Gianna's frequent visits.

"Only once did I experience a strange sensation," Mariuccia recalls sadly, "a kind of disturbing presentiment... but I quickly brushed it aside."

> A few days before the end of Gianna's pregnancy, she came to my home for a visit. After she came into the house, she went upstairs; I forget why. Dino, my oldest son, was sit-

ting, as he often did, on one of the steps. "Where are you going, Aunt Gianna?" he asked her. "Upstairs, but I'm coming right back," she answered. Then she stopped. She caressed his head and said to him, "Perhaps this is the last time that you will see Aunt Gianna."

I have asked myself countless times why she said those words, especially to a child. Perhaps she wanted to give me a hint of something she didn't have the courage to tell me directly.

In a small book Pietro wrote to keep Gianna's memory alive in the hearts of her children, he offers one of the most touching testimonies to this courageous woman:

> With incomparable strength of spirit and unaltered commitment, you continued your mission as mother and physician until the very last days of your pregnancy.
>
> You prayed and meditated.
>
> I remember how your usual smile and your usual satisfaction over the beauty, health, and liveliness of our children often veiled a deep worry. You feared that the little baby in your womb would be born suffering. You prayed so hard that this would not happen.
>
> Many times, you asked for my pardon if you were a worry to me. You told me that you needed love and understanding more than ever. Not once, in all those long months, did you say a word to me about your awareness, as a doctor, of what could happen to you. Surely, this was because you did not want me to suffer.
>
> I worried about how you were quietly putting our home in order—every corner, every drawer, and every personal object—as if you were leaving on a very long journey. But I did not dare to ask you why.

Gianna with Pierluigi and Mariolina

Pietro Molla attributes Gianna's actions to her great love lived in a heroic manner:

> You made your sacrifice for the sake of charity, because of your sense of maternal responsibility, because of the supreme respect you had for that pregnancy, for the child in your womb who, in your view, had the same inviolable rights as...the other babies you had carried and given birth to, as well as those you might have had in the future—all of them were gifts from God.
>
> In the months following the operation, you suffered so greatly without any complaint! You prayed so much that the baby might be born healthy and normal and both your lives might be saved. It was your complete trust in the Lord's providence, your certainty of the efficacy of prayer, and your abandonment to the will of God that gave you strength and support during that long, anxious wait.
>
> You loved our three precious children no less than you loved the baby in your womb. For all those months you prayed to the Lord, to Our Lady, and to your own mother that the right and guarantee to life for the baby in your womb might not require the sacrifice of your life, that you would be spared for the sake of our children and our family.
>
> At the same time, if the Lord's will were different, if it were not possible to save both lives, you explicitly asked me to make sure that the child's life be saved.
>
> With your decision, you offered the holocaust of your life. And you offered it with the anguish of a wife and a mother who must leave behind her children and family and everything dear that God had given you. You offered your life asking, in your humility and faith, and with the fullness of your trust in God, that you be spared the fear

> that your sacrifice might be an act of injustice toward our children and toward me.
>
> You would not have carried out the heroic act of saving the life of your unborn baby if you had considered it an act of injustice toward our family or a betrayal of the morality that you saw as one with all of God's laws. You knew that your maternal obligation to raise, educate, and form our children was no less serious than the duty to safeguard their coming into the world after their conception. You knew very well that no one could equal your maternal love in raising, educating, and forming our children. But in your humility, you trusted that the Lord would make up for the absence of your visible presence. You believed that you would not be acting unjustly either toward our children or toward me, as you accepted the Lord's will, knowing that I, even in my distress, shared your faith and love.

Mother Emma Ricetti, a Canossian sister, echoes this testimony:

> When her pregnancy imposed suffering and risks on her life, she followed the right and holy way that knows no compromise, secure in God's help, ready for any sacrifice.
>
> This generosity prepared her for her final heroism, all the more significant because she was a qualified physician of rare competence and knew all the risks and the minimal or nearly non-existent possibility of saving herself if she persisted in her will to save her baby. Yet, she persisted without ever doubting, secure in her offering, ready for sacrifice, even though she felt it in the depths of her being.

On the afternoon of April 20, Good Friday of 1962, Pietro accompanied Gianna to the hospital in Monza. Gianna was serene and did not appear at all worried. She knew she was nearing the end of a nine-month-long painful journey, yet she was full of hope.

Savina remembers watching Gianna leave the house saying, as usual: "Take good care of the children." Pierluigi, Mariolina, and Lauretta were excited—Mama would come back with a new little brother or sister. Gianna tenderly kissed them good-bye and got into the car.

At the hospital in Monza, she was admitted to obstetrics on the second floor.

After an unsuccessful night trying to induce labor, Dr. Vitali consulted Ferdinando and they decided to deliver via cesarean section. They explained the situation to Pietro, and he gave his consent.

At 11:00 A.M. on April 21, a beautiful baby girl was born. Pietro named his new daughter Gianna Emanuela. Shortly after she awoke from the anesthesia, the exhausted Gianna was able to hold her little girl in her arms. "She gazed on her for a long time in silence," Pietro remembers. "She clasped her to herself with unutterable tenderness. She caressed her lightly, without saying a word."

15
Her Total Gift

Tremendous suffering followed the brief moments of joy Gianna experienced after her baby's birth. As her postpartum pains continued to increase and her temperature rose, Dr. Vitali and the medical team worked anxiously to resolve these complications. Diagnosed with septic peritonitis, Gianna received all of the then-known treatments: antibiotics, blood transfusions, and injections. Nothing helped.

Pietro did not leave Gianna's side for an instant. He held her hand and gently caressed her damp brow. Others stayed with Pietro in his vigil: Ferdinando and his wife and the nuns at the hospital took turns at her bedside; Father Marella remained with her until the end.

In spite of her intense pain—she had to bite down on a handkerchief to suppress her cries—Gianna asked that she not be sedated. She wanted to remain conscious. She spent the long days of her agony without complaining. When Sister Virginia arrived, a dialogue of courage and Christian acceptance unfolded between the two sisters. Gianna confided in her sister: "Ginia, how differently we judge things from a deathbed…certain things that used to seem so important now appear so useless."

Gianna called out for her mother, asking her for the strength to bear her intense pain. She murmured the names of her children. She felt that she would soon leave them and she worried about them. Yet, she also found the strength to ask for the Eucharist, to call out to Jesus for help, to clasp a crucifix and kiss it and whisper, "Oh, if Jesus were not here to console us at times like this…!"

On Tuesday night, she began to slip into a coma, but then seemed to shake off unconsciousness to utter anguished words of love to her husband.

As Gianna's condition deteriorated, Dr. Vitali banned all visitors, allowing only Virginia to remain in the small hospital room where Gianna was completing her sacrifice. Gianna suffered from this seeming abandonment on the part of everyone she loved. Virginia tried to reassure her and help her to feel the warmth of the love and prayers of her husband who, just outside her door, was living his own grief in silence. Zita, Ferdinando, Father Giuseppe, and Father Marella were also there with him. Sister Virginia talked to Gianna about her children and told her about the many friends who came to the hospital to ask about her and pray for her. The two sisters prayed together for courage and acceptance.

Wednesday and Thursday passed in endless hours. Gianna was growing more exhausted and weak, but she patiently accepted all the medical treatments that the doctors administered.

The beautiful mosaic in the chapel at Mesero that depicts Our Lady of Fatima with Gianna, Mariolina, and Teresina, Pietro's sister

Pierluigi, Mariolina, and Lauretta had no idea that their mother would not come home to play with them or to listen to their lively chatter. Their little sister, Gianna Emanuela, spent the first few days of her life peacefully in the nursery of the maternity ward. As she grew older, her father would tell her of her mother's great love: Gianna's readiness to give her life for her. Gianna gave her life as Jesus taught in the Gospel: "There is no greater love than to lay down one's life for a friend" (cf. John 15:13). Twice, Gianna had declared this complete, unreserved love: first in September 1961, when she asked that her pregnancy be saved despite her awareness of the risk she was taking, and again when she explicitly asked Dr. Vitali to save her baby's life before her own.

On Friday, Gianna fell into a coma from which she would not awaken. Pietro knew his wife's wish would be to return to their home. On Saturday morning, Gianna was brought by ambulance to the house where she had lived, for so few years, as a happy wife and mother.

She was laid in the bed she had shared with her beloved husband, while her children slept in the next room. Pietro did not dare to waken them.

He remained alone beside his wife who died peacefully at 8:00 A.M. on Saturday, April 28, 1962. Gianna was not yet forty years old.

The chapel in Mesero where Blessed Gianna, Mariolina, and Pietro's relatives are buried

The four Molla children at Courmayeur in 1963,
the year after their mother's death

16

After Gianna's Death

After Gianna died, Pietro found himself having to be both father and mother to his four children, though he was not alone. His mother and his sister, Sister Luigia, and Gianna's sister Zita helped him to raise the children after the example of their mother's life.

Only two years after Gianna's death, another great sorrow fell upon the Molla family: six-year-old Mariolina died following a very brief illness.

Pierluigi attended the elementary school directed by his aunt, Sister Luigia. He completed his secondary school and classical degree at the College of San Carlo in Milan. Later, he earned his doctorate in economics and commerce at Bocconi University. He is now married and the proud father of a daughter, Ortensia Carlotta, who was born in 1989.

Lauretta and Gianna Emanuela (or Giannina, as she is called at home) attended elementary school in Ponte Nuovo. They completed their secondary education and degree in Magenta. Lauretta went on to earn her doctorate in political science. Gianna Emanuela became a doctor and surgeon.

Gianna with Mariolina in San Vigilio, Bergamo (1957)

Lauretta and Gianna Emanuela live with their father in Milan and lead quiet, Christian lives.

Of the Beretta family, only two brothers and two sisters are still living: Father Alberto, the Capuchin missionary doctor; Giuseppe, the priest and engineer of the diocese of Bergamo; Sister Virginia, the physician and Canossian Missionary; and Zita, the pharmacist.

After thirty years as director of the St. Francis Hospital in Grajau, Brazil, Father Alberto suffered a nearly total paralysis and had to return to Italy. He has lived in the old family home in San Vigilio, Bergamo, under Zita's tender care since 1981.

Father Giuseppe has worked as the curator of diocesan art work for more than forty years in the Chancery Office of Bergamo.

After many years of missionary work in India, Sister Virginia is now a physician at the Clinic of Paul VI Social Center of Acilia, near Rome.

« Appendix A »

Gianna's Life Touches the World: What Others Have Said

Lauretta Molla, age 15

In an essay written on January 31, 1974

The clouds covered the sky, but they allowed the sun's rays to filter through; however, these were not enough to warm the air. A light breeze moved the new buds; bunches of daisies, primroses, and violets could be seen here and there in the meadows, in such profusion that everything looked painted.

It must have been a rather nice day, at least for other people; for me, however, it was terrible. I was only three years old, and I did not really understand the meaning of all those lit candles, of women in black, and of all the crying.

Mama was lying on her bed, pale and cold as ice. She was no longer breathing.

What impresses me the most was her dedication to being a real mother, conscious of her duties toward her family, wanting to provide us with a moral formation and

Gianna with Lauretta sledding at Courmayeur (1960)

a good education. Although her work kept her busy for most of the day, she tried to stay with us as much as possible, for, in the early years of life, children absolutely need the presence of a mother to guide them and watch over them. She carried out her work as a doctor so carefully and happily, and she particularly liked to care for children—especially those in greatest need. I think that she continued her task as a mother within her office. Among the thousands of things she had to think of, she gave importance not only to her own children, but also to the other children around her who needed her help.

I remember the wonderful vacations we spent with her in the mountains, where we were all together when Papa could join us. Those were the finest days, when the whole family was together enjoying the beauties of creation, running happily through the mountains, and leaving unpleasant matters aside.

I will never forget the Christmas of 1961, the third and last that I spent with my mother. She had lovingly prepared me for the celebration of the birth of Jesus. To this day, I can remember the poetry I recited for Mama and Papa—I laugh when I remember the comical way I recited it. At the same time, a profound sadness comes over me; I miss those days and I wish so much to live with her again.

Of all the feelings I experience, the one that stands out most is the deep admiration I feel for a mother—my mother—who gave her life for her child. She truly preferred to leave behind her joyful existence so that the baby she was bringing into the world might also experience the joy of living and thanking God for his creation.

It is certain that she had great courage, and I believe that few mothers would have done the same thing. However, I am also sure that her example, which many people have come to know, has served to comfort mothers who have found themselves in a similar situation.

Finally, I can say that I am truly proud of having had such a courageous mother who lived as God wanted her to live, and who served humanity by her example and by her works.

I feel that she is always close to me, particularly during this time of my formation, and that she is helping me as if she were still in this life.

Pierluigi Molla

Sunday, October 31, 1999, Gianna's son gave this speech at the ceremony of blessing and dedication of the stained glass windows in the Newman Center Chapel at the University of Toronto, Canada.

I am deeply grateful to Father Thomas Rosica and the Newman Center of Toronto and would like to express my gratitude...for having chosen the beautiful and endearing image of my mother, now Blessed, to be among "this cloud of witnesses," holy ones of this century, particularly Blessed Pier Giorgio Frassati, Blessed Brother André, Franz Jägerstätter, Archbishop Oscar Romero, and Georges and Pauline Vanier, as well as St. Teresa Benedicta of the Cross, St. Thérèse of Lisieux, and Mother Teresa of Calcutta....

Already in March 1986, the witness and message of my mother had spread to Newfoundland, where the *Natural Family Planning Association* printed in their newsletter

Gianna holds her beloved children Pierluigi and Mariolina

a brief biographical profile of mom, titled, "A Portrait of Love." In December 1990, in the city of Vancouver, *Gianna House,* a pro-life support center was opened for women. We were touched and consoled to know of the richness of the witness and message of my mother, even before the cause for her beatification was concluded.

Then almost six years ago, in December 1993, we were moved with great joy that the *Friends of Gianna Society* had begun in Vancouver. In February 1997, we were again deeply touched to read in the "Family Life" section of the weekly *British Colombia Catholic,* the beautiful article by Marie Luttrell, titled "For Courage, Faith, and Humility," which focused on the roots of my mother's choices and exemplary life.

On April 24, 1994, in St. Peter's Square in Rome, His Holiness Pope John Paul II proclaimed Gianna Beretta Molla, *mother of a family,* "Blessed." From that moment until today, the number of my mother's friends has grown....

Today we have the privilege of seeing my mother honored by all those present, especially by so many young people and all of those who minister to them at the Newman Center Catholic Mission at the University of Toronto. This Center truly represents what my mother lived and died for: Jesus Christ and the Gospel of Life.

There are three reasons why I think it is so important that the image of my mother has been placed in the Chapel of the Newman Center:

First, the witness of my mother was a *hymn to life,* to a love for life and all the beautiful things in life. It was a hymn to a faith lived with joy and nourished by the Eucharist and by prayer. Even in her medical profession, she knew how to see Jesus in her neighbor whom she loved and served with such great generosity.

Second, my mother knew how to live her daily earthly existence with simplicity, balance, and constant service—all in a beautiful harmony—as a young student and professional, as a woman and wife and mother. Her generous commitment to and involvement in Catholic Action and to the St. Vincent de Paul Society, along with her *joie de vivre,* was crowned with her love for the piano, painting, tennis, mountain climbing, skiing, the symphony, theater, and travel.

Third, even from her earliest youth, my mother fully accepted the gift of faith and an explicitly Christian education, which she received from her excellent parents who, in their vigilant wisdom, knew how to accompany her in her human and Christian growth. Whether it was in her youth, primary or secondary education, or in her university courses in Medical School, Gianna received from exemplary priests, religious, and wise professors, a pedagogical formation that was clearly in harmony with Cardinal John Henry Newman's idea of a university in which theology, the arts, and sciences would be taught in dialogue with one another. In her daily living, my mother was faithful to the pedagogical formation she received and she knew how to transpose that formation into a joyful living of the Gospel, all the while being a brilliant example of true love and respect for life, even to the summit of the love that Jesus teaches in the Gospel: *laying down one's life for one's friends.*

On April 25, 1994, the day after her beatification, in his address to an audience of pilgrims who had come to the ceremony, Pope John Paul II defined my mother's life with these words: *"What a heroic testimony her life was...a true hymn to life!"*

Dr. Gianna Emanuela Molla

Sunday, October 31, 1999, Gianna's daughter gave this speech at the ceremony of blessing and dedication of the stained glass windows in the Newman Center Chapel at the University of Toronto, Canada.

I am very honored and moved to be here today with all of you and I thank with all my heart Father Tom Rosica, his staff, the parishioners and friends of the Newman Center present at this important ceremony. Three days ago, when Father Tom showed me the windows for the first time and I saw my mother smiling, I was filled with joy and felt so pleased because I have always imagined her this way, and know that the message of her life could not be better represented.

Every moment of her entire existence was a real testimony of Christian love and faith, which she lived concretely and with joy in her everyday life: as young girl, fiancée, wife, mother, and doctor. She always trusted in divine providence and she has crowned her exemplary life in the name of a love without measure. She is always with me and since the momentous day of April 24, 1994 [her beatification], I have felt myself part of an ever-growing family of so many people throughout the world who, like me, pray to her, confide in her, and feel close to her. I believe that this is also the design of divine providence: now I shall never be alone.

Pietro and Gianna Emanuela with her uncle, Father Alberto, and Aunt Zita in the woods of San Vigilio, Bergamo, 1989

Dear Mom, I ask you to fill me and all those who suffer and are in difficulty with your own strength of soul, your hope, your courage to live life to the full. Protect and help all mothers, their families, and all who turn to you and entrust their needs to you.

I now invite you to pray with me the prayer to my mother:

GOD, you who are our Father, we give you praise and we bless you because in Gianna Beretta Molla you have given and made known a woman who witnessed the Gospel as a young woman, as a bride, as a mother, and as a doctor. We thank you because through the gift of her life, we learn to accept and honor every human being.

You, Lord Jesus, were her privileged reference. She was able to know you in the beauty of nature. As she questioned her choice of life, she was in search of you and of the best way to serve you. Through her married love, she became a sign of your love for the Church and for humanity. Like you, Good Samaritan, she stopped at the side of every sick, small, and weak person. After your example and for your love, she gave herself entirely, generating new life.

Holy Spirit, font of every perfection, give also to us the wisdom, intelligence, and courage exemplified in the life of Gianna, and through her intercession, may we be able to put ourselves at the service of every person and to grow in the way of love and holiness in our personal, family, and professional lives. Amen.

Cardinal Albino Luciani, Patriarch of Venice (Later Pope John Paul I)

In an article published in Messagero di S. Antonio

Cardinal Colombo, the Archbishop of Milan, has recently opened the process of beatification for Gianna Beretta Molla, a medical doctor who specialized in pediatrics. In her fourth pregnancy, she faced an operation with the dilemma: "...either we save you or we save your child." "I prefer that you save the life of my little one," she answered, well aware of what was in store for her.... She gave birth to a very healthy baby girl on April 21, 1962, but she died a week later, having sacrificed herself....

Paul VI

September 23, 1973, Rome

...[Gianna Beretta Molla] a mother of the diocese of Milan who, in order to give life to her baby, sacrificed her own life as a deliberate immolation.

Cardinal Giovanni Colombo, former Archbishop of Milan

September 24, 1966, on the occasion of the dedication of the elementary school of Ponte Nuovo in memory of Gianna Beretta Molla

Before such a radiant example that certainly can never be forgotten by the Church, one's deepest desire is to remain silent, to meditate, to admire, and to pray. And the desire comes into our hearts to become worthy of such souls whom the Lord undoubtedly sends to us on earth to bring us a message.

He has told us that there is no greater love than for one to give his life for a friend. Gianna Beretta Molla had the courage to set out on the path of this greatest love and therefore was able to imitate more closely the sacrifice of the Lord Jesus.

And if there were a desirable way to perpetuate her memory, it seems to me that this idea of dedicating a school to her is truly a fine one. For all of the boys and girls who will be educated here will carry in their own spirit, as it grows in life, something of her maternal quality, and will feel in some way that they are her sons and daughters.

May she bless them all from heaven, and may she aid and comfort her family, her spouse, and all of us. We feel that she is close, and in her memory, we invoke the Lord's blessing.

Cardinal Carlo Maria Martini, Archbishop of Milan

Conclusion of the cardinal's Easter meditation at the Cathedral of Milan, March 21, 1986

I take the liberty of calling to mind the example of Gianna Beretta Molla, because this morning we concluded the diocesan process for her beatification.

Gianna Beretta Molla was a wonderful woman.... She was a woman who loved life. She was a wife, the mother of a family, a physician, and an exemplary professional. She gave her life so that the mystery of the dignity of life would not be violated.

Hers was an existence truly illuminated by the mystery of the washing of feet and by the mystery of the crucifix. Witnesses state that she was a very ordinary woman, who practiced her medical profession very well. She loved to be among people and she radiated her joy and enthusiasm around her.

Yet, her trust in Providence was very strong. What strikes me the most is her firmness in saving her pregnancy to the detriment of her own life. She acted decisively and simply, gazing at the Crucified Lord.

Hers was an existence illumined by the mystery of Christ who serves in the washing of feet, and who serves in joy, communicating joy and peace to the apostles.

A watercolor portrait of Gianna Beretta Molla (rendered by the artist, Anna Pavesi) displayed in St. Peter's Square for her beatification

⁂ Appendix B ⁂

Gianna Beretta Molla—a Saint?

December 24, 1962: The provincial administration of Milan presents to Gianna Beretta Molla's family a gold medal in her memory, with the following statement:

> A diligent and generous collaborator of the ONMI Clinic of Magenta, inspired by a Christian spirit consistent with profound faith in eternal values, while a mother of three young children, she did not hesitate to sacrifice her own young life to bring her last child into the world. Her name gives witness to and exalts the sublime heroism of all mothers, and arouses deep sentiments in the hearts of all who recognize the unfailing principles of civilization.

Also present at the ceremony was the future Pope Paul VI, Cardinal Giovanni Battista Montini, Archbishop of Milan, who was deeply touched by Gianna's heroic sacrifice.

September 24, 1966: The Board of Education of Milan re-names the elementary school of Ponte Nuovo di Magenta in honor of Gianna Beretta Molla. Cardinal Giovanni Colombo, Archbishop of Milan, presides and offers a memorial speech.

November 6, 1972: Cardinal Giovanni Colombo, having gained the favorable opinion of the Bishops Conference of Lombardy, promotes the cause for the beatification of the Servant of God Gianna Beretta Molla, and requests the compilation of informative acts and documents.

April 11, 1978: Cardinal Giovanni Colombo and the sixteen members of the Bishops Conference of Lombardy petition Pope John Paul II for the introduction of the cause for the beatification of Gianna Beretta Molla.

In the Postulatory Letter, Cardinal Colombo and the bishops implore the glorification of this wife and mother, defining her as "a highly timely model for our world that is led to disregard and reject the right to life." The letter continues:

> [S]uch a mother, a martyr for the love of God, and in obedience to his commandment, which forbids killing, gives witness to and exalts the sublime heroism of a Christian wife and mother who, in her respect for all life, which is always God's gift to humanity, sacrifices her own young life in order to say "yes" to the Christian duty of love. It is this example of a wife and mother that we, the archbishops and bishops of Lombardy—in the name of our faithful—wish to see proposed to the entire Church.
>
> Today, through selfishness and violence, it has become too easy to kill in every way, be it hidden or open. In this world, which is prone to call for and introduce legislation that legalizes abortion, the Servant of God Gianna Beretta Molla becomes a courageous example of Christian life. This example of lay holiness, lived in the matrimonial state, as Vatican Council II teaches, will encourage many

Christians to seek God in the marital state. The fame for exemplary Christian behavior, which Gianna Beretta Molla enjoys, is effective testimony of this. The life and the conscious sacrifice of Dr. Molla illuminates the importance of the Christian family, of Christian schools, of Catholic Action in the formation of a Christian personality, and in communicating some principal guidelines to which a Christian must subordinate life itself, just as Dr. Molla consciously did.

April 27, 1978: The Archdiocesan Chancery of Milan sends the compiled acts and documents to the Congregation for the Causes of Saints.

February 8, 1980: The Congregation authorizes Cardinal Giovanni Colombo to issue a decree for the introduction of the cause.

March 15, 1980: Pope John Paul II confirms the authorization for the introduction of the cause, and the Congregation for the Causes of Saints grants the *nulla osta* [there is no obstacle].

April 28, 1980: By the decree of Cardinal Carlo Maria Martini, Archbishop of Milan, the cause for the beatification of the Servant of God Gianna Beretta Molla is officially introduced.

June 30, 1980–March 21, 1986: The process investigating the life and virtues of the Servant of God, following the usual *Institution* by the Congregation, is conducted at the Chancery of Milan, 158 sessions for the deposition of forty-eight witnesses, including five called by reason of their office.

September 29, 1980–January 5, 1984: A Rogatorial Process of twenty-one sessions to collect seven testimonies takes place in Bergamo. Among the witnesses are seven priests, nine religious women, a number of Gianna Beretta Molla's collaborators in Catholic Action and in her medical profession, and the Servant of God's husband, brothers, sisters, and other relatives.

April 11, 1986: Father Bernardino da Siena, the Postulator of the Cause, delivers the Cognitional Process of Milan and the Rogatorial Process of Bergamo to the Congregation for the Causes of Saints, furthering the request for opening the cause. Both Processes were compiled into four volumes totaling 2,570 pages. Beyond the process depositions, abundant documentation was compiled, examined, certified, and attached. This documentation is comprised of writings, memories, statements, written correspondence, and testimonies given by relatives and strangers who wrote of special favors attributed to Gianna Beretta Molla's intercession.

April 12, 1986: The *Decree of Opening* is issued.

November 14, 1986: The Congregation issues the *Decree of Validity* and begins the definitive examination of the life and virtues of the Servant of God Gianna Beretta Molla.

July 6, 1991: The Congregation for the Causes of Saints confirms the heroic virtues of Gianna Beretta Molla by the decree signed by Pope John Paul II.

∝ Appendix C ∞
The Final Step

After the pope signed the decree confirming the heroic virtues of Gianna Beretta Molla, one final step remained before the Church could officially proclaim her a blessed: the validation of the miracle attributed to her, which occurred in Grajau, Brazil.

In 1977, in the hospital Father Alberto had helped to build in Grajau, a young woman lay dying. She had given birth to her fourth child, a stillborn, by cesarean section. A very serious complication caused a rectal-vaginal fistula that was inoperable in that facility. The nearest hospital with the means necessary to attempt to save her life was in São Luis, a city more than 600 kilometers away. To transport the young woman there was nearly impossible, and her condition was worsening.

A nurse in the ward, Sister Bernardina of Manaus, was very worried about her patient, and she turned in prayer to Gianna Beretta Molla to ask, through her intercession, that the dying mother be healed of her illness and thus avoid the dangerous journey to São Luis. Gazing on a small picture of the Servant of God, she prayed: "You who are Father Alberto's sister, make this fistula heal and keep this woman from having to travel to São Luis...."

Sister Bernardina invited two other nurses to join her in this supplication. According to the sick woman's testimony, not only did her pain subside immediately, it also completely disappeared.

When the nurses notified the hospital physician, he was surprised to find that the woman's condition was no longer urgent; it was no longer even necessary to transport the young mother to São Luis. The fistula had completely healed....

The compilation of the proofs for this miraculous event was very laborious. Three processes had to be held in Grajau between November 1981 and October 1987 before the depositions of all persons knowledgeable in the matter were finally gathered.

On May 22, 1992, the Special Congress of the Congregation of the Causes of Saints met in Rome. It consisted of the Promoter General of the Faith, functioning as president, along with six theological consultants. They discussed and evaluated the miracle attributed to Gianna Beretta Molla's intercession. The case under review required the approving votes of all seven participants of the Special Congress.

Each one of the participants in the commission submitted their first vote in writing. After a brief discussion, during which they took into account the unanimous evaluations and conclusions of the Medical Consulting Board, they expressed their approval of the preternatural quality of the healing. All acknowledged the sufficiency and validity of the juridical and theological proofs, and recognized as a strict nexus of cause and effect, the concomitance between the invocations addressed to the Venerable Servant of God Gianna Beretta Molla—and only to her—and the prodigious event of the healing.

Regarding the category of the phenomenon, all considered it a third-degree miracle, that is, an instantaneous, complete, and lasting cure unexplained by medical science.

The Beatification

On April 24, 1994, during the Year of the Family, Pope John Paul II beatified Gianna Beretta Molla. Present for the celebration in St. Peter's Square were her brothers and sisters, her husband Pietro, and her surviving children: Pierluigi, Lauretta, and Gianna Emanuela. Praising Gianna for her heroic virtue in sacrificing herself "to give life to the child in her womb," the pope offered her as a model for all mothers, saying:

> A woman of heroic love, an outstanding wife and mother, she gave dedicated witness to the demanding values of the Gospel in her daily life. By holding this woman up as an example of Christian perfection, we would like to pay homage to all brave mothers who dedicate themselves to their own family without reserve, who suffer in giving

> birth to their children, and who are ready to make any effort, to face any sacrifice, in order to pass on to them the best of themselves.... We thank you, heroic mother, for your invincible love! We thank you for your intrepid trust in God and in his love. We thank you for the sacrifice of your life. Today, Christ is restoring to you the gift you gave him. Indeed, he has the power to give back the life you gave him as an offering.

At the Maracana Stadium in Rio de Janeiro, Brazil, during the Second World Day of the Family in October of 1997, Pope John Paul II listened tearfully as Gianna Emanuela Molla offered some words to the audience, which ended with the following prayer:

> Dear Mama, thank you for having given me life two times: when you conceived me and when you permitted me to be born.... My life seems to be the natural continuation of your life, of your joy of living, of your enthusiasm; I discover my life's full meaning in dedicating myself to whoever lives in suffering.
>
> Dear Mama, intercede always for all mothers and all families who turn to you and entrust themselves to you.

During an audience with the members of the Beretta and Molla families (April 25, 1994), Pope John Paul II warmly embraces Gianna Emanuela

At the end of the audience, Pope John Paul II and Cardinal Martini pose with the family members: Fr. Alberto (seated); behind him, (r) Fr. Giuseppe, (l) Zita, and behind them, Mother Virginia. To the pope's

left: Gianna Emanuela, Lauretta with Pierluigi's daughter, and Pietro Molla; (behind the pope) Pierluigi and his wife

Following the beatification ceremony, Gianna Emanuela—with her father, Pietro Molla, and her sister Lauretta—gives Pope John Paul II a rosary that belonged to her mother, Blessed Gianna

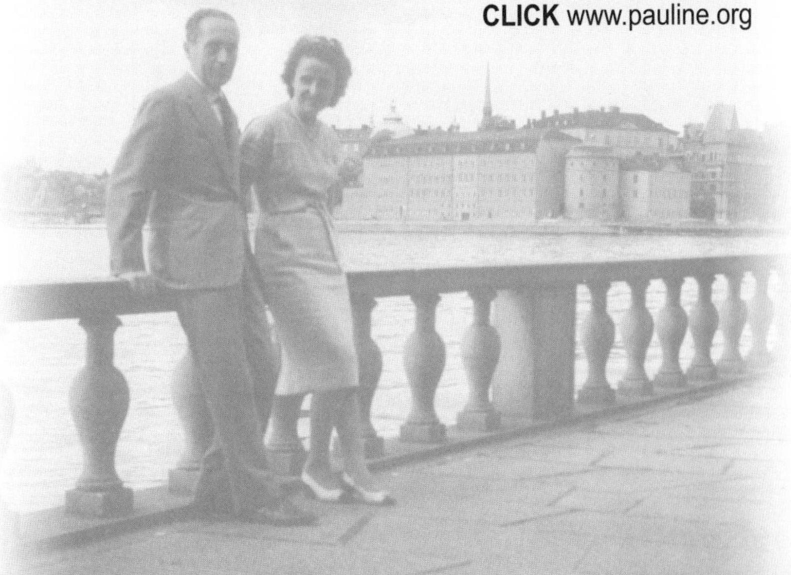

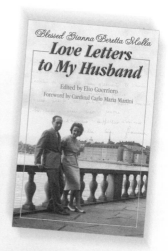

The Daughters of St. Paul operate book and media centers at the following addresses. Visit, call or write the one nearest you today, or find us on the World Wide Web, www.pauline.org

CALIFORNIA
3908 Sepulveda Blvd, Culver City, CA 90230 310-397-8676
5945 Balboa Avenue, San Diego, CA 92111 858-565-9181
46 Geary Street, San Francisco, CA 94108 415-781-5180

FLORIDA
145 S.W. 107th Avenue, Miami, FL 33174 305-559-6715

HAWAII
1143 Bishop Street, Honolulu, HI 96813 808-521-2731
Neighbor Islands call: 800-259-8463

ILLINOIS
172 North Michigan Avenue, Chicago, IL 60601 312-346-4228

LOUISIANA
4403 Veterans Memorial Blvd, Metairie, LA 70006 504-887-7631

MASSACHUSETTS
Rte. 1, 885 Providence Hwy, Dedham, MA 02026 781-326-5385

MISSOURI
9804 Watson Road, St. Louis, MO 63126 314-965-3512

NEW JERSEY
561 U.S. Route 1, Wick Plaza, Edison, NJ 08817 732-572-1200

NEW YORK
150 East 52nd Street, New York, NY 10022 212-754-1110
78 Fort Place, Staten Island, NY 10301 718-447-5071

OHIO
2105 Ontario Street, Cleveland, OH 44115 216-621-9427

PENNSYLVANIA
9171-A Roosevelt Blvd, Philadelphia, PA 19114 215-676-9494

SOUTH CAROLINA
243 King Street, Charleston, SC 29401 843-577-0175

TENNESSEE
4811 Poplar Avenue, Memphis, TN 38117 901-761-2987

TEXAS
114 Main Plaza, San Antonio, TX 78205 210-224-8101

VIRGINIA
1025 King Street, Alexandria, VA 22314 703-549-3806

CANADA
3022 Dufferin Street, Toronto, Ontario, Canada M6B 3T5 416-781-9131
1155 Yonge Street, Toronto, Ontario, Canada M4T 1W2 416-934-3440

¡También somos su fuente para libros, videos y música en español!